Scottish History and Mythology

An Enthralling Journey Through Scotland's Past and Legendary Myths

Free limited time bonus

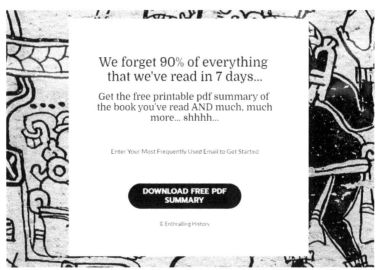

Stop for a moment. We have a free bonus set up for you. The problem is this: we forget 90% of everything that we read after 7 days. Crazy fact, right? Here's the solution: we've created a printable, 1-page pdf summary for this book that you're reading now. All you have to do to get your free pdf summary is to go to the following website: https://livetolearn.lpages.co/enthrallinghistory/

Or, Scan the QR code!

Once you do, it will be intuitive. Enjoy, and thank you!

Table of Contents

Part 1: History of Scotland

An Enthralling Overview of Important Events and Figures

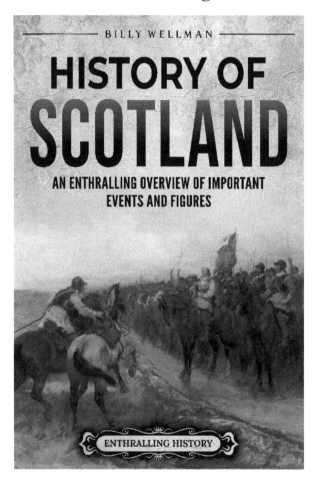

Introduction

East of Edinburgh, along the coastline where the Firth of Forth meets the North Sea, is a small seaside town called North Berwick. In late October 2023, the coast was smashed by huge waves and sea surges. A section of the town's sea wall crumbled from the force, leaving a sixteen-foot-wide gap. Luckily no one was injured, and, apart from the seawall, no property was damaged.

What makes this an interesting moment in Scottish history is that the wall was over four hundred years old. North Berwick, the town, has existed since the thirteenth century. Throughout the Middle Ages, it was the southern station of a ferry used by pilgrims heading to and from the Shrine to Saint Andrew. When New Berwick replaced several water lines, archaeological excavations uncovered hut circles and middens that are at least 2,000 years old. Archaeologists also found Iron Age cist burials, a unique type of stone coffin that can be found at many Scottish sites.

All of this is not to say that North Berwick, despite being a very picturesque town, is extraordinary. Actually, it's the opposite. Scottish history is permanently stamped into the very ground that modern Scotland stands on. History is ubiquitous in Scotland, unescapable from the perspective of someone living in, say, the United States.

Yet, we don't necessarily think of Scotland as an "old" country like Egypt or Greece. Not even, perhaps, as old as England or Spain. This might have something to do with the mighty Roman Empire, which came to Egypt, Greece, Spain, and England but never to Scotland. In the Romans' view at least, Scotland was never properly "civilized." Scotland, like Ireland, most of Germany, and all of Scandinavia, was *terra incognita* to the empires of the Mediterranean.

Scotland's history might start somewhat obscurely, but over time this relatively small nation became one of the most influential countries in the world. Still, it remains something of a mystery to the outside. This book will peel back the legends to reveal the complex truth lying underneath. It will delve into the past of this nation perched amidst the gray sea and among the crags and heather to expose a history that is not only astonishing but certainly enthralling.

Chapter 1: Ancient Beginnings — Picts, Gaels, and the Formation of Alba

The nation of Scotland is made of the northern third of the island of Britain as well as 790 surrounding islands, which include the archipelagos of the Shetland Islands, Orkney Islands, and the Inner and Outer Hebrides. The geography of Scotland is distinguished by the Highland Boundary Fault, which separates the country into the Lowlands of the east and south and the Highlands of the north and west. The highest mountain is Ben Nevis, which reaches 4,413 feet above sea level.

In the south, the Central Belt, which lies between two large bays called the Firth of Clyde and the Firth of Forth, is home to most of the population, concentrated in the largest city (Glasgow) and the capital (Edinburgh). The northernmost point of Scotland (and the United Kingdom) is Out Stack, an uninhabited island among the Shetland Islands. It is nothing more than a rocky outcrop, but someone traveling north from the island would not meet another landmass before reaching the North Pole.

The longest river is the River Tay, which runs from its source for 120 miles before it empties into the North Sea. Freshwater bodies of water are typically called lochs, with the largest being Loch Lomond. Though Scotland is on the same latitude as Labrador, Canada, its weather is mild thanks to the North Atlantic Drift.

The earliest evidence of humans in the area now called Scotland dates from about 12,000 BCE. These were only a few flint artifacts. More stone tools from a few thousand years later were discovered, indicating that humans began to populate Scotland when the last Ice Age was ending and the glaciers that had previously covered the British Isles were receding. These Mesolithic (Middle Stone Age) people were hunter-gatherers. Gradually, the people of Scotland made significant changes in their modes of living and settlements and became Neolithic (New Stone Age) farmers who deforested land for crops and livestock.

On the main island of the northern Orkney archipelago, two sites point to the existence of incredibly advanced societies in remote locations. First, there is Maeshowe, which was built around 2800 BCE and is a mound burial. Under the mound are tombs and passageways made of crafted flagstone. The most striking element of Maeshowe is the central chamber, which is aligned in such a way that the entire room is illuminated only during the winter solstice. Also on the main island is the site of Skara Brae, a small stone village occupied from 3180 to 2500 BCE. Skara Brae consists of ten clustered houses also made of flagstone with stone hearths, beds, and cupboards. A primitive sewer system featured toilets in each house that flushed into a drain that went into the nearby ocean. Both sites are older than the pyramids of Giza. The inhabitants ate seafood and probably grew barley.

One of the houses, House Eight, lacks beds and cupboards and instead is made of small cubicles. The presence of bones found at that location suggests it might have been a work site for flint tools. Other artifacts found at the site include carved stone balls. These balls, which typically measure about two and three-fourths inches in diameter, have been found all over Scotland and in other places in Britain and Ireland. The exact purpose of these balls is unknown, but they could have been used ceremonially, as weapons, or to move large stone monuments.

One of the key features of these Neolithic sites in Scotland is the presence of cairns. The term "cairn" comes from the Scottish Gaelic word *càrn*. It is a constructed pile of stones used as a marker, sometimes indicating a burial. "Chambered cairns" are burial monuments that consist of a large chamber over which cairns have been placed. Chambered cairns have been found in Ireland, Wales, and England, but the majority are in Scotland, suggesting cultural similarities between these nations. These cairns are often found near Neolithic settlements like Links Noltland, Barnhouse, and Rinyo in the Orkney Islands and Balfarg in the town of

Glenrothes. However, neolithic remnants can be found all over Scotland, including the Calanais and Kilmartin Glen standing stones and recumbent stone circles found in the northeast.

Unlike the inhabitants of Skara Brae, most Neolithic Scots lived in wooden houses or huts. These houses, of course, do not remain, so stone sites like Skara Brae or Knap of Howar on Papa Westray are the most prominent examples of Neolithic buildings. Knap of Howar might just be the oldest preserved stone house in Northern Europe and was the site of a homestead. Scots on the Orkney Islands did not have much timber, so they used stones to build, which is why the Orkney Islands seem to have so many Neolithic sites.

On South Ronaldsay in the Orkneys, a farmer digging in 1958 discovered what is now called the Tomb of the Eagles. In it were found 16,000 human bones from at least 324 individuals, as well as talons and bones from twenty birds, predominantly white-tailed sea eagles. Evidence suggests that the tomb was used by Neolithic people for thousands of years.

All these sites suggest that Neolithic Scots were advanced engineers, astronomers, and mathematicians.

Around 2000 BCE, the Stone Age gave way to the Bronze Age in Scotland, and the archaeological record shows a decline in large stone buildings. In the Orkneys, people were buried in smaller *cists*, and the culture of the area was changing. While many of the hallmarks of Neolithic culture spread south from Scotland, Bronze Age culture, denoted by the working of metal, spread north from Europe to Scotland.

One of the earliest Bronze Age finds was discovered when some workmen were blasting a knoll behind Bonar Bridge and found the so-called Migdale Hoard. This collection of jewelry dated from 2000 to 1150 BCE and included a bronze ax head, bronze bangles and anklets, and jet and cannel coal buttons.

At the Forteviot Bronze Age tomb, discovered in 2009, an individual was buried in a *cist* on a bed of quartz and birch bark with a leather bag and a bronze dagger with gold work around the hilt. The tomb dates from between 1950 BCE to 2100 BCE. The site is near Perth, a centrally located city on the River Tay, which has been the site of settlements in prehistoric times, including during the Bronze Age.

A very significant site that dates to about 2000 BCE is at Cladh Hallan on the island of South Uist in the Outer Hebrides. There researchers found four skeletons that had been buried in a peat bog, then removed and stored inside a structure, only to be buried two centuries later. These bodies would have been mummies, preserved around the same time as King Tutankhamun in Egypt. It is particularly interesting and mysterious as to why the bodies were purposely preserved in the bog and then buried hundreds of years later. DNA analysis of the mummies has revealed that they are made of at least six different individuals.

Bronze Age Scots show the first signs of metallurgy and wheeled transport (including chariots). They built large mortar-free or dry-stone structures like brochs, which were usually double-walled stone towers whose exact purpose remains a mystery. They also built Atlantic roundhouses, which were, as the name implies, circular stone buildings with conical thatched roofs. In fact, brochs are considered complex roundhouses as opposed to the simple roundhouses found in Orkney.

These types of structures were carried into the Iron Age, which began in the first millennium BCE. In a field in Stirlingshire in 2009, an amateur metal detectorist discovered the most significant Iron Age metallurgical find in Scotland. It consisted of four golden torcs, a type of necklace that dated from 300 to 100 BCE. It is called the Stirling Hoard. Later investigation revealed that the torcs had been buried inside a roundhouse, perhaps for ceremonial purposes. The torcs exhibit extremely fine craftsmanship, and at least one of the torcs shows a Mediterranean influence in style. This suggests a link between Scotland and Southern Europe, but more evidence is required to substantiate this theory.

The first known written record of Scotland comes from a Greek explorer named Pytheas from the colony of Massalia (Marseille, France). Like many ancient writers, Pytheas' writing does not survive to modern times except when he is mentioned by other, later authors. The exact dates of his voyage into Northern Europe are unknown but are estimated to have been around 350 BCE. Besides seeing Scotland and the British Isles, Pytheas was also the first ancient writer to mention the Arctic and the midnight sun. Pytheas' descriptions of the people of Britain are lacking in detail, mentioning only that they lived in thatched huts, baked bread, and fought from chariots. When he reached the northern part of Scotland, he called the islands Orcas, from which the name Orkney was derived.

By 79 CE, Scotland was said to be the home of the "Caledonii" and the massive, primeval Caledonian Forest found in the writing of Pliny the

Elder. This directly resulted from a significant change in Scottish history: the Roman invasion of Britain. The Roman invasion was not just dramatic for the people of Britain but brought the hallmarks of the Roman Empire. Before the arrival of the Romans, Scottish history was told only by archaeological evidence, but after the Romans, written accounts were sent back to Rome, where they were kept for thousands of years. These accounts are always from the Roman perspective and push the Roman agenda, which said that conquest was the right of Rome and beneficial to the conquered. The empire brought civilization, and any resistance to this was a sign of barbarousness and savagery. The ancient Scots, or Caledonians as they were called, certainly appear in Roman writings as savage barbarians.

The invasion of Britain was the brainchild of Emperor Claudius I, who, in 43 CE, needed to show his strength and correct his predecessor's mistake in giving up on an invasion of Britain. The invasion promised glory—and, perhaps more importantly, wealth—to not just the imperial family but the average soldier. The Romans were about 40,000 strong when they landed on the coastline of Southern England. The Romans had some early successes. Claudius landed to take place in the final push of one of the battles and left after sixteen days. He claimed victory, and the Senate awarded him a triumph, calling for triumphal arches to be built and honoring him with the name "Britannicus," though he never used it. Despite Claudius' theatrics, the invasion of England was much longer and harder fought. Still, Britannia became a Roman province and fell under imperial control. However, the land farther north was still unconquered. The Romans traveled into the land they called Caledonia under the command of Gnaeus Julius Agricola, who was responsible for much of the conquest of England.

In 79 CE, the Romans pushed through Scotland quickly with little resistance. However, they failed to inflict heavy casualties on the Caledonians because the natives simply disappeared into the wild forests, or "wilds," as the Romans called them.

Finally, according to the historian Tacitus (Agricola's son-in-law), the Romans met the Caledonian Confederacy in battle at a place called Mons Graupius in northern Scotland in 83 CE. The Caledonians were commanded by a chieftain named Calgacus. These people most likely spoke Scottish Gaelic, a language of the Gaels, an ethnolinguistic group comprising people in Ireland, Scotland, and the Isle of Man. The name Calgacus might have come from the Gaelic word *calgach*, meaning "prickly" or "fierce." This chieftain is the first named Caledonian in history, but he did not last for long. He led his people to defeat at the hands of the Romans. However, Calgacus only appears once in Tacitus' records, where he gives a speech and then is no longer mentioned. This has led some to speculate he was an invention of the writer.

While Agricola certainly dealt the Scots a heavy blow, he did not knock them out, and two-thirds of their army evaded capture in the forests and mountains. Mons Graupius, which might have been in Aberdeenshire, was not the definitive battle Agricola hoped for. His army reached as far as the northern tip of Britain or perhaps no farther than Loch Ness or Moray Firth; it is unclear. Regardless, the Romans eventually turned south, having failed to subjugate the Caledonians. In 85 CE, Agricola was recalled to Rome by Emperor Domitian, who might have been jealous of Agricola's victories. Regardless, Agricola never returned to Britannia.

Several brochs appear to date to the period of Agricola's invasion. In Melrose in the Scottish Borders, Agricola constructed a large Roman fortification. These structures certainly agree with the idea that brochs might have had a military use and that this was a time of invasion and resistance.

A Roman garrison was established in Scotland after Agricola's invasion, totaling 25,000 soldiers. However, Agricola's unknown successor was either unwilling or unable to follow through with the conquest of Caledonia.

Tacitus' description of Agricola's victories is undoubtedly biased and stirring, but he could not conceal the fact that after Agricola's invasion, Scotland remained free and "wild." By 87 CE, just three years after Agricola's victory, Roman forts and camps were dismantled, and the Roman Empire drew back to the Stanegate road between Tyne and Solway Firth, south of the border between Scotland and England.

In 122 CE, the construction of Hadrian's Wall began. The wall was built between Wallsend on River Tyne in the east to Bowness-on-Solway in the west in Northern England. The wall was seventy-three miles long and about eight to ten feet thick in places. It is believed to have been about twelve feet tall.

Emperor Hadrian had wanted to solidify the empire's borders to combat growing revolts and raids from outsiders into Roman-conquered areas. Caledonians, like barbarians elsewhere, would cross into Roman territory (England) to steal and destroy. The intention was that the wall would stop this. According to the archaeological evidence, it succeeded. Very few Roman goods are found in Scotland from this period. Accounts suggest there was a sort of "no-man's-land" beyond the wall that was kept cleared and patrolled by Roman soldiers. No one got in or out. The Caledonians, cut off from their southern neighbors, continued much as they had been while England grew increasingly Rome-like.

The Iron Age Caledonians who lived beyond the wall were farmers and shepherds who grew grain and raised pigs, sheep, and cattle. They settled in small towns or villages, where residents lived in timber buildings with thatched roofs. Higher-ranking families sometimes lived in stone roundhouses or perhaps in brochs. They lived in numerous identifiable tribes ruled by a chieftain, who sometimes had an allegiance to another chieftain, thereby creating confederacies like the one that fought Agricola. They spoke a Brythonic Celtic language and were a Celtic people who worked metal and were excellent horsemen. Their weapons were made of wood, metal, and leather.

According to the Romans, there were sixteen different tribes in Scotland. Twelve of them lived north of the Forth-Clyde isthmus in what is considered Northern Scotland. In later Roman maps, the Caledonii are shown living in the Central Highlands, southwest of a tribe called the Vacomagi. Aberdeenshire was the home of the Taezali tribe, and Fife was the home of the Venicones.

After Hadrian's death in 138 CE, his successor, Antonius Pius, launched a vigorous assault to retake the Lowlands and establish a defensive line below the River Forth. The newly appointed governor of Brittania, Quintus Lollius Urbicus, led the new invasion, and within a few short years, the Lowlands were back under Roman control south of a new imperial line—the Antonine Wall across the Forth-Clyde isthmus. The wall was not built of stone but was an earth rampart with a ditch in front of it. It featured sixteen forts at regular intervals along its forty-mile length, housing 6,000 garrisoned troops. Yet, after ten years, it was briefly abandoned, and ten years later, it was permanently evacuated. After Antonius Pius' death in 161 CE, the northern border shrank back to Hadrian's Wall once again.

Things remained this way until, sometime between 180 and 184 CE, the Caledonians stormed the wall and crossed it. The Romans could not take back the wall, but it was a sign of trouble in the north. By the third century, the Romans faced not only the Caledonians but also another group called Maeatae from territory in Stirlingshire. Both groups appear to have been amalgamations of several smaller tribes that had been absorbed into larger groups, perhaps by force or by alliance.

In 205 or 206 CE, these two groups launched an invasion into Britannia. The governor asked for assistance from the emperor, Septimius Severus, who arrived in 208 CE at the head of a large army. The barbarians waged a guerrilla war but were subdued for a time until the emperor fell ill and died and his son, Caracalla, became emperor. There were plans to try again to take the north by force, but they were abandoned for being unfeasible, and Caracalla made peace with both groups. This was the last attempt by Rome to take Scotland; they would never again attack the people of the highlands and the glens.

However, for the next century, Rome maintained a semblance of order by holding public gatherings in places north of Hadrian's Wall where locals could air their grievances and Romans could keep an eye on any potential troublemakers. These meetings were held at *loci*, which is simply Latin for "places." Each *locus* was held at a place of importance for the natives. The assembly at the *Locus Manavi* (The Place of the Manau district) was gathered around a sacred rock. This name survives in the city and county of Clackmannan, which is Scottish Gaelic for "The Stone of the Manau."

It is not known how often these meetings took place or exactly how they were conducted, but they helped provide a certain amount of peace in the area for generations. Then, in 297 CE, there is mention of two barbarian groups that were particularly troublesome to the Romans. One was the *Hiberni*, who were the inhabitants of the island of Ireland. The others were a group never before mentioned: the *Picti*, or the Picts. Later writings indicate that the Caledonians were the Picts, or it might have been the other way around. Modern historians believe that the Caledonians Confederacy split in two and one group appeared on Roman maps as the *Dicalydones*, a name that indicated the split. The Picts were described by the Roman historian Ammianus Marcellinus in 360 CE as two separate groups: the Dicalydones and another group called the Verturiones. Therefore, the Picts appear to have been a new nation formed from the Caledonian Confederacy and the Verturiones, but the exact nature of this nation is still largely unknown.

The Picts almost certainly didn't call themselves that. Instead, their name for themselves remains unknown. *Picti* was soldier slang for

"Painted People," indicating body painting or tattooing. The Romans casually identified anyone north of Firth of Clyde as being Pictish, but it is not clear that these people represented a unified nation or even if they all spoke the Celtic language of Pictish. Still, anyone from the Highlands and the islands of Scotland would have shared certain Pictish characteristics, including body decorations of blue tattoos, religious beliefs, and, most likely, a shared language.

To get a good idea of how widespread the Pictish language was, an excellent source is Claudius Ptolemy's world map, made in about 150 CE. Ptolemy shows the British Isles on the map and gives many tribal names and place names. They were names of Celtic origin given to the Romans, who Latinized them. The massive Isle of Skye is given the name *Scetis* on the map. Linguists believe this was derived from a so-called P-Celtic language, which included Briton and Pictish but excluded Gaelic.

The Pictish language, which is mostly unknown, shared similarities with Welsh, as well. The Welsh prefix "aber," which means "river mouth," can also be seen in Scottish names like Aberdeen and is believed to have been Pictish in origin.

Over the next centuries, the Picts, along with Saxons from Germany and Irish people, attacked Britannia with various levels of success. The Romans, meanwhile, were struggling to hold their empire. In 410 CE, when Britons requested aid from Rome, they were told to fend for themselves. The Roman presence in Britannia was over, and many of the soldiers and citizens, who were already indistinguishable from the Britons around them, simply joined a new era in which British kingdoms arose.

The German Angles, Saxons, and Jutes came to what would be England first as mercenaries and later settled, eventually revolting and pushing the Britons out of their native lands. The Anglo-Saxons, as we call them, called themselves *englisc,* from which is derived "English."

The two tribes who lived in the Lowlands of Scotland, who identified more with the Britons than the Picts, formed their own kingdoms, providing a barrier that kept the Picts in the north. The Votadini tribe became the Gododdin kingdom and built their fortress on Castle Rock in Edinburgh. The Damnonii created a kingdom centered on Dumbarton and what they called Alt Clut or "Clyde Rock" in the Clyde Valley.

This began a period that started in 500 CE or so and is sometimes called the Early Medieval period in Britain. The Roman Empire had left, but their influence was still apparent in the recording of histories in Latin and the spread of Christianity, though both were not embraced by the Picts.

At this time, the Picts were identified as a unified culture and society, though separated into organized kingdoms. They lived in a place called Pictland and erected standing stones, which featured unique symbols and acted as monuments. They were erected by the order of Pictish chieftains, who may now be referred to as kings. These symbols appear on stone at Skye, Perthshire, Orkney, and Shetland with an amazing uniformity. What the symbols meant remains a mystery.

During this Early Medieval period, another kingdom developed—or, more accurately, reemerged—in what is now Argyll on the western coast of Scotland. It was called Dál Riata, and it was not just confined to Scotland but spanned the Northern Channel to Antrim in Northern Ireland. The people of this kingdom spoke Gaelic and were culturally known as Gaels.

The origins of this kingdom are shrouded in legend. Early writers speak of the three sons of Erc, who conquered *Alba*, the Gaelic name for Scotland, but there is little archaeological evidence for an Irish invasion. The people in Argyll were separated from the rest of Scotland by the Highlands, so it is possible they connected culturally with the people of Northern Ireland and created a kingdom founded on this relationship. In fact, modern scholarship and genetic research show that the Scottish Gaels were native to Scotland and not of Irish origin. They were most likely the descendants of the Epidii, a tribe the Romans were aware of in the second century.

The Scottish Gaels were among the first people in Northern Scotland to convert to Christianity after contact with Saint Columba, who crossed from Ireland to convert the peoples of Northern Britain. The Venerable Bede, writing in the eighth century, called the nation of the Gaels *Scottorum*. This is presumably from the Roman custom of calling speakers of Gaelic *Scotti*. From this developed another name for the Gaels of Dál Riata, the "Scots."

The Scots were often at odds with their neighbors, the Picts, and several wars were fought for dominance of the Highlands. The king of Dál Riata, Áed Find (or Áed the White), fought the Pictish king, Ciniod, in 768 CE in the Battle of Fortriu, but the outcome of the battle has since been lost.

Yet, in the final decade of the eighth century, a new group appeared on the shores of Scotland, and they would have a great impact on the Scots and Picts. They were the Vikings. These raiders from Norway appeared to attack at random and disappear, leaving death and destruction behind them. Eventually, it became clear that these were not just raiders but armies of occupation. In 839 CE, the Picts and Scots combined their forces to drive out the invaders, but they were soundly defeated, and the kings of both nations were slain in the battle. This left a vacancy on both thrones. In 840 or 841 CE, the crown of Dál Riata was set on the head of the previous king's son and heir, Cináed mac Ailpin. After a series of short-reigned kings, in 850 CE, the Pictish crown fell to a conqueror who had seized the throne. His name was none other than Cináed mac Ailpin.

Chapter 2: The Emergence of the Scottish Kingdom—MacAlpin to Canmore

Kenneth MacAlpin (also known by the Gaelic name Cináed mac Ailpin) is credited as the unifier of the Scottish Kingdom. The writers of the Irish annals call him *Rex Pictorum*, or "King of the Picts," yet they do not explain how or why he got this title. Historians presumed it was based on the fact that MacAlpin had been a Gaelic conqueror who took control of Pictavia, but this is neither supported nor denied by the documents. It is equally as possible that MacAlpin was a legitimate claimant to the throne of the Picts. The Pictish nobility was known to have contained Gaelic families.

It is not clear whether Kenneth I, as he is sometimes called, united the two kingdoms in 850 CE or much earlier in 842 CE. It was the presence of the Vikings, who raided Pictish and Scottish lands indiscriminately, that drove the two kingdoms together, and MacAlpin, who might have been part-Scot and part-Pict, was the culmination of this merger. He may have put in his bid for the Pictish throne in 842 CE, but the process of defeating his rivals was not complete until 850 CE. At this point he became the first king of a unified kingdom often given the Gaelic name Alba; eventually, it would be known as Scotland. The first kings of the "House of Alpin" were still called "King of the Picts."

KENETH I.

A modern idealized depiction of Kenneth MacAlpin.
https://commons.wikimedia.org/wiki/File:Kenneth_MacAlpin_of_Scotland_-_the_first.jpg

One of Kenneth's first actions was to move a collection of relics of Saint Columba (primarily bones) from the island of Iona to the town of Dunkeld in Perthshire just north of the town of Scone. To appreciate the significance of this action, one must understand better who Columba was. Born in Ireland in 521 CE, Columba (or in Gaelic, *Colum Cille*) was the grandson of Irish King Niall. In 563 CE, legend says that he left Ireland as a form of self-imposed exile. A bloody battle had resulted from his refusal to hand over a copy of the Gospels he had supposedly copied illegally. Full of remorse for the deaths he had caused, Columba traveled to the tiny island of Iona because it was out of sight of his native land. There, Columba began building an abbey and is said to have banished snakes, frogs, cows, and women from the island.

Columba was a man of letters and a missionary. His monastery at Iona became the premiere center of learning in the Kingdom of Dál Riata, and he is said to have spread Christianity to the Picts. One of the many miracles attributed to him is the banishing of a "water beast" into the River Ness, which some believe is the first reference to the Loch Ness monster.

Columba, Iona, and the relics associated with the saint became extremely important to the people of Ireland and Scotland. Kenneth's repositioning of the relics to a more central location in his new kingdom shows the beginning of a Scottish national identity. Not all of Columba's relics went to Dunkeld. Some were sent to Ireland, where Columba (or Colum Cille) was also revered.

By the time Kenneth had brought the kingdoms of Dál Riata and Pictavia together, the Irish parts of Dál Riata were their own kingdoms ruled by their own kings. Kenneth's focus was firmly held on the island of Britain. He fought the Britons of the kingdom of Strathclyde, also known as Alt Clut, in the valley of the River Clyde and invaded the region of Lothian in the Kingdom of Northumbria on six separate occasions.

He also had to constantly contend with the Vikings. In fact, he most likely removed the relics at Iona because life on the island was no longer possible with persistent Viking raids. From Iona, he also brought a coronation stone on which the kings of Dál Riata had been crowned and placed it in the royal residence in the town of Scone. It was thereafter known as the Stone of Scone and would be used in the coronation of the kings of Scotland.

Kenneth died in 858 CE, just a few years after securing his new kingdom. According to the Gaelic tradition of "tanistry," the crown then fell to Kenneth's brother, Donald I, also known as Domnall. Donald reigned for just four years before he also died. He was followed by Causantín mac Cináeda, which can be read as Constantine, son of Kenneth. He is often known as Constantine I.

Viking activity was at its height during Constantine's reign. While the "Great Heathen Army" of Vikings were attacking the Anglo-Saxons, the Northumbrians, and the Welsh, other groups of Vikings were attacking farther north from bases they had established in Ireland. Two Viking leaders who might have been brothers, Amlaíb and Auisle, defeated a portion of the Pictish kingdom and obtained tribute and hostages in 866 CE. Later sources claimed that Auisle killed Amlaíb over the former's wife, who was said to be the daughter of Cináeda. However, the accuracy of this story (and whether the wife was the daughter of Kenneth and sister to King Constantine) is completely unknown.

In 877 CE, Constantine was captured and executed by Viking raiders. He was succeeded by his brother Áed, who reigned for less than a year before dying in mysterious circumstances. The next king was Giric, possibly the son of Donald and nephew of Kenneth. He was known as "Mac Rath," or "Son of Fortune." There is scant information on Giric, and it is not clear if he was the King of the Picts alone or the King of Alba. He might have co-ruled with Eochaid ab Rhun, who was also King of Strathclyde and a grandson of Kenneth MacAlpin through his mother. Legend claims that Giric slew Áed, which led to Eochaid's ascent to the throne. It is possible that Giric and Eochaid ruled together or that both claimed the throne of Alba in opposition to each other.

In 889 CE, either Giric died or Eochaid and he were deposed by Domnall mac Causantín, son of Constantine I, who would be nicknamed *Dásachtach*, "the Madman." His name is anglicized as Donald II. He may have been the first king to take the title "King of Alba," or it might have been one of his successors.

By this time, the Picts, decimated by the Vikings, had been won over to Celtic Christianity through missionaries like St. Columba and had abandoned their Brythonic language for Scottish Gaelic. They did not disappear, but outside pressure and time appeared to have forged the Gaels and Picts into the singular Kingdom of Alba. Most historians consider this the end of the process begun by Kenneth and the beginning of what would become the Kingdom of Scotland.

Donald II either died or was deposed by his cousin, Constantine II, grandson of Kenneth and son of Áed, in 900 CE. However, Alba did not extend over all of modern-day Scotland. To the south were the kingdoms of Northumbria and Strathclyde, which were constantly shifting alliances between each other, the English kingdom, and the Welsh. To the north and west of Alba was the Earldom of Sudrland (Sutherland), an old Viking region where the invaders had become largely "Gaelicized."

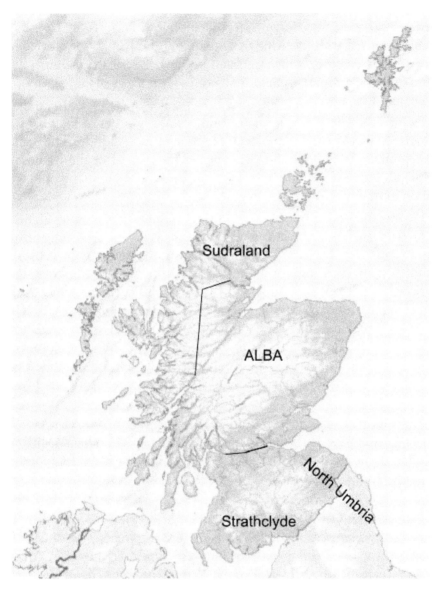

Map of Scotland in 900 CE.
Eric Gaba, NordNordWest, Uwe Dedering, CC BY-SA 3.0
<https://creativecommons.org/licenses/by-sa/3.0>, via Wikimedia Commons; Labels added by
author; https://commons.wikimedia.org/wiki/File:Scotland_relief_location_map.jpg

Constantine II's reign was largely focused on dealing with incursions from the Vikings, also known as Norsemen. He was, for a time, allied with the growing Kingdom of England in the south. Then, King Athelstan, the first truly English king, invaded southern Alba in 934 CE, though it appears no battles were fought. In retaliation for this invasion, Constantine II allied himself with the King of Dublin and the King of Strathclyde, but they were defeated by King Athelstan in the Battle of Brunanburh in 937 CE, a defining moment in the forging of English national identity.

Constantine II reigned for forty-three years. In 943 CE, he abdicated and joined the Culdees, a monastic and eremitical order in Fife that would come to be associated with the Cathedral of St. Andrew. The Culdees were popular in Ireland and Scotland and were part of the traditions of Celtic Catholicism in which priests were allowed to marry and could engage in business to produce wealth.

He was succeeded by Malcolm I (Máel Coluim mac Domnaill), the son of Donald II. The later chronicles say that Malcolm took an army into Moray and "slew Cellach." It is not clear who Cellach was or if his death resulted in the province of Moray, made from part of the great Pictish kingdom of Fortriu, becoming part of Alba. This seems possible as those in the ruling House of Moray are often described as *mormaers*, a Gaelic name for a regional ruler. Malcolm allied with Edmund I of England and appears to have invaded parts of Strathclyde and Northumbria in conjunction with the Anglo-Saxons. Then, in 954 CE, he was killed either in battle or by the treachery of Moravians in retaliation for his previous invasion.

Malcolm was succeeded by Indulf mac Causantín "the Aggressor," the son of Constantine II. Indulf might have conquered Lothian at this time, bringing the town of Edinburgh into Alba. He died in 962 CE, possibly fighting Vikings. Malcolm I's son, Dub mac Maíl Coluim, then became king.

Dub was known as "the Vehement." He reigned for only five short years and was most likely killed in battle against Cuilén, the son of King Indulf, who wanted the throne for himself. King Cuilén also only reigned for five years before being killed by Britons in 971. His assassin might have been Rhydderch ap Dyfnwal, a Cumbrian who might have been the son of Dyfnwal ab Owain, the King of Strathclyde. According to some accounts, Rhydderch killed Cuilén after the king had raped the Briton's daughter.

The next king of Alba was Amlaíb mac Illuib, another son of King Indulf, but his reign was disputed and short-lived. It seems he lost his bid for the throne and most likely his life to Kenneth II, son of Malcolm I.

King Kenneth's nickname is given as "the Fratricidal." The *Chronicles of the Kings of Alba* were compiled during Kenneth II's reign.

The feud that had grown between the two branches of the Alpínid dynasty continued. Kenneth, wanting to secure succession for his descendants, sought to change the rules of succession in Alba. However, this was discovered by his cousin and next in line to the throne, Constantine, son of Cuilén. Before Kenneth could change the laws governing succession, Constantine had him killed by deceit and became the next king, Constantine III, in 995 CE.

Two years later, Constantine III was killed in battle fighting Kenneth III, son of King Dub, who became king in 997 CE and reigned until 1005. King Dub was succeeded by his cousin, the son of Kenneth II, King Malcolm II. In 1018, Malcolm secured Lothia under Scottish rule. In that same year, the King of Strathclyde died, and, thanks to marriage alliances, Malcolm II's grandson, Duncan, sat on the throne of Strathclyde.

In 1034, Duncan succeeded his grandfather as King of Alba, which now stretched south into England. In 1040, Duncan was killed in battle by Maelbeatha, or Macbeth, the *mormaer* of Moray. Despite popular opinion, Macbeth appears to have been a wise monarch who ruled for seventeen years. At this time, Macbeth was defeated in battle by Duncan's elder son, Malcolm III, also known as "Canmore," meaning "Big Head" or "Great Chief."

Malcolm III had grown up in England, and his second wife was the English Princess Margaret, who had taken refuge in Scotland after the Norman invasion of 1066. Margaret tried to lead the Celtic Church of Scotland to the Roman Catholicism of her homeland, where priests practiced vows of celibacy and poverty. Margaret would be canonized for her work by the Catholic Church.

Norman William the Conqueror eventually invaded Scotland and forced Malcolm to pay homage to him. In 1093, Malcolm was killed in battle by a Norman. Malcolm's brother, Donald Bane, claimed the throne but was challenged by Malcolm's son, Duncan. Both were eventually overthrown by an Anglo-Norman force that put Duncan's half-brother, Edgar, on the throne. Edgar was succeeded by his brother Alexander and then by his brother David I, "the Saint."

David did much to improve the lives of the Scots. In a purely medieval sense, he "modernized" what had long been a relatively backwater European kingdom. When he died, the throne passed to a young son, whose reign did not last long. The next king was William "the Lion," who ruled for forty-eight years. At first, he blundered by losing much to the English after a terrible defeat, but eventually, he regained much that he had lost.

The next king was Alexander II, who continued the relatively peaceful and prosperous years of his previous two predecessors. However, Alexander II died in 1249 of illness while attempting to bring the Kingdom of the Isles (the Isle of Man, the Hebrides, and the islands of Clyde) away from their allegiance to Norway. He left behind a seven-year-old son, also named Alexander.

Alexander III, upon becoming an adult, brought the Isle of Man and the Western Isles under Scottish control in 1266 and continued the relative peace and prosperity of his father. He had three children by his first wife, Margaret, daughter of Henry II of England. However, all three children and his wife predeceased him. He declared his granddaughter, Margaret the "Maid of Norway," his successor. He married a second time to Yolande of Dreux, in France. However, he died while riding his horse in a storm in 1286. His new wife was pregnant, but she gave birth to a stillborn child. Thus, the Maid of Norway, a Norwegian princess who was only one year old, was the heir presumptive of Scotland. However, she too died in 1290 on her way to Scotland. This sudden weakness in Scotland's succession proved a perfect opportunity for one of the great villains of Scottish history, King Edward I of England.

Chapter 3: The Struggle for Independence

In Scotland, the news of the Norwegian princess' death caused incredible turmoil. There were now more than a dozen claimants to the throne. The two strongest were Robert de Brus (Bruce) and John de Bailleul (Balliol). Both were of Anglo-Norman origin with estates in England and Scotland. Both were descendants of David I through his youngest son. Both were known by Edward I as they had both served in his army. However, it was believed that Balliol would be the more docile of the two and easily managed by King Edward.

In 1291, with Edward watching, a gathering of nobles announced that Balliol would be given the crown. Edward then immediately demanded that Balliol pay homage to him and recognize England's feudal superiority over Scotland. Balliol would be expected to come to London when called to answer any claims against him and should provide funds for England's defense cost. The new king was also expected to join in a planned invasion of France. Though Balliol might have been as docile as Edward believed, England's demands were too much. Balliol formed an alliance with France and planned to invade England in 1296.

King Edward, called Edward Long Shanks (due to his height of six foot two inches) and "the Hammer of the Scots," was a shrewd king above all else. He had already conquered Wales when he set his sights on Scotland. When he helped facilitate the election of John Balliol as king in what is sometimes called the "Great Cause," he had already decided on a complete conquest of the kingdom. In fact, he had planned for Balliol's refusal of his demands and was prepared to meet the Scottish invasion.

Two days after Balliol entered England, Edward's forces were crossing into the borderlands of Scotland. There, Edward was met by a contingent of Scottish nobles who supported him, many of whom had estates in England, including Balliol's rival Robert Bruce. Balliol took all of Bruce's lands and gave them to his brother-in-law Red John Comyn. Edward marched on Berwick, the most prosperous city in Scotland at the time. He sacked the city and killed many of its inhabitants. Then, at Dunbar, he met and defeated Balliol, who renounced his crown and eventually withdrew to France.

Edward continued, taking Edinburgh, Stirling, Perth, Elgin, and several castles. When he returned to Berwick, a host of nobles and knights signed the "Ragman's Roll" declaring Edward king. Edward left for London, taking the ancient Stone of Scone with him.

Then, in the spring of 1297, a young Scottish knight known as William Wallace got into an altercation with some English soldiers in a marketplace in Lanark. With the help of a girl (some say was his wife), he escaped, but the girl was caught and put to death by the sheriff of Lanark. That night, Wallace returned and killed the sheriff, becoming an outlaw.

People must have seen in Wallace a chance to get revenge against the hated English. Within weeks, he was leading a movement of national resistance. The movement gathered supporters, and in September 1297, an English army under the command of Viceroy John de Warren, Earl of Surrey, faced off against a band of warriors from all over Scotland led by William Wallace. The Battle of Stirling Bridge would become a crucial battle in the First War of Independence and a source of pride for Scots everywhere.

Wallace and his ablest lieutenant, Sir Andrew de Moray, were arrayed on the north bank of the River Forth. The English outnumbered the Scots and were better trained and more experienced. The English army began to cross the Stirling Bridge over the River Forth. This meant that only a small number of English soldiers could face the Scots as the battle began. The Scots used long spears to trap the English cavalry that approached them. Many soldiers and horses tried to cross the Forth but drowned in the muddy waters. The bridge eventually collapsed under the weight of English who could not move forward or back in the confusion. The Scots slaughtered the soldiers remaining on their side while the rest of the army looked on in horror.

The English retreated to Berwick. It was a great victory for Wallace, but Andrew de Moray had been killed in the action. In the summer of 1298, King Edward defeated Wallace at Falkirk, though Wallace escaped. He remained a hunted man until 1303 when he was caught and brutally executed by the English.

It seemed, for a moment, that Scotland would remain subject to the English king, but some nobles were getting restive under English rule. Among them were Robert Bruce, son of the previous claimant to the throne, Red John Comyn, who now led the former Balliol faction, and Sir Simon Fraser of Tweeddale, who had fought alongside William Wallace.

Bruce and Comyn met in Greyfriars Kirk (Church) at Dumfries in 1306. A quarrel broke out, and Bruce stabbed Comyn, killing him. This was not a particularly newsworthy event since rival nobles killed each other often. What made it notable was that the killing had been done in a church and was thus blasphemous. In one act, Bruce had made blood rivals of the Comyns and assured the Catholic Church would oppose his plans to rid Scotland of the English and put himself on the throne.

Despite this, Bruce went to Scone in March 1306, raised the royal standard, and crowned himself the new King of Scotland. In response, Edward sent an English army into Scotland, which defeated Bruce at Methven. Many of Bruce's allies were captured and executed. He went into hiding in the Scottish Islands and possibly Norway. Slowly, Bruce gathered strong allies, including the earls of Lennox and Atholl, Angus Og of Clan Donald, and the powerful Campbell and Maclean clans. He returned to the kingdom and conducted guerilla warfare, achieving victory at Louden Hill.

Edward I decided to lead a great army to subdue the Scots, but, at the age of sixty-eight, died at Burgh-on-Sands in Cumbria, England. England's heir was the king's son, Edward II, but he was not the man to carry on his father's invasion. Edward Longshanks had left his son a kingdom in financial and political difficulties with too many enemies and not enough friends.

The king's death was a turning point for Bruce and Scotland. Robert Bruce defeated his Comyn enemies and was secretly recognized as king of Scotland by the king of France. In 1310, the Church of Scotland decided to support Bruce despite his excommunication by the pope. Bruce invaded and devastated northern England, sacking Durham and

Hartlepool. He drove the English garrisons out of Perth, Dundee, Dumfries, Roxburgh, and Edinburgh.

By 1314, Edward II was finally compelled to meet Bruce's army at Stirling, but he made the mistake of letting Robert choose the ground. After a few hours of fighting through marshlands and uphill, the English were fleeing. By 1318, Berwick, the last English stronghold, had fallen and the Scots were again free from English rule.

Edward II tried to invade Scotland again in 1322, but he was chased back into Yorkshire so rapidly that he didn't have time to gather his baggage. Edward tried to get the new pope, John XXII, to confirm the excommunication of Robert Bruce. This caused the Scottish nobles to address themselves to the pope directly. "We fight," they told him, "not for glory, nor riches, nor honor, but only for that liberty which no true man relinquishes but with his life." The Pope appears to have been somewhat swayed as he lifted Bruce's excommunication.

In 1327, Edward II was deposed by his wife, and his young son, Edward III, took his place on England's throne. A peace treaty, the Treaty of Edinburgh-Northampton, was signed between the two kingdoms in 1328. In it, England recognized Scotland as a separate kingdom and Robert Bruce as the rightful king.

By this time, the kings of Alba had long been using a different title, but the exact time the change was made is unclear. By the reign of David I in 1124, the ruler was known as *Rex Scottorum* or "King of the Scots," but this was sometimes written as *Rex Scotiae,* or "King of Scotland."

King Robert I had ruled as King of the Scots—focusing on the people instead of the land—since 1306, but the English did not recognize him as such until 1328. He did not live long enough to enjoy the new peace. In June 1329, Robert I, who had fought so hard to free Scotland and had been suffering from a serious disease (possibly leprosy), died at the Manor of Cardross near Dumbarton. His five-year-old son, already married to the English Princess Joan, became King David II. King Robert's daughter, Margery, had married a nobleman named Walter FitzAlan, the Hereditary High Steward of Scotland. This brother-in-law of the new king was often known as Walter Stewart or, in later forms, Stuart. The regent was Bruce's nephew, Thomas Randolph, Earl of Moray.

When a group of disgruntled Scottish nobles, urged on by Edward III, landed at Fife with the intent of putting John Balliol (Toom Tabard)'s son, Edward Balliol, on the Scottish throne, Randolph went to meet them but died before the battle commenced.

The next regent was another of Bruce's nephews, the Earl of Mar, who was defeated and killed in a night attack. The invaders marched to Scone, where they crowned Balliol. Before the usurper could do much damage, an army led by Archibald Douglas and Andrew Moray of Bothwell drove him out of the kingdom.

Edward III took this moment to strike and marched to retake Berwick, which he did. Scottish nobles switched sides and allied with the English, and the Lowlands were taken once again. David II was forced to flee to France, and the regency now fell to Bruce's grandson and the son of Walter Stewart, the seventeen-year-old Robert Stewart. Stewart took command, and with the help of the French, recaptured Perth. By 1340, Scotland was clear of the English north of the River Forth. The next year, David II returned from France and took control of the country from Stewart.

The English were distracted by a war with France, but in 1346, the King of France asked his ally for a diversion, and David II responded by leading an army into England. He was beaten at Neville's Cross and taken prisoner, where he remained at the court of Edward III for the next twelve years. Robert Stewart was once again regent.

In 1355, the French again asked for a diversion. Robert responded by recapturing Berwick while the English were defeated by William Douglas at Nesbit Muir. Edward III tried to retaliate by invading Lothian, but his troops were forced to withdraw, tired and demoralized.

Edward tried a new approach and offered to release King David II to his people for the hefty price of 100,000 marks. But David was a poor king, and Scotland was now a poorer country. David, who was on good terms with Edward, offered to surrender to England and make Edward's son his heir. The Scottish nobles were outraged. When David died in 1371, the kingdom was given not to the English but to Robert Stewart, the first Stewart king.

Chapter 4: The Stuart Dynasty

King Robert II had been a competent regent and proved to be a competent king—at first. His reign, from 1371 to 1390, was long enough and his missteps few enough that Scotland enjoyed another span of relative peace and prosperity. One of his key acts was to secure from the Scottish Parliament the hereditary passing of the crown from father to son or daughter.

The Parliament was a relatively new institution that had evolved from the king's council into a legislative body of three estates: the first estate of prelates (archbishops, bishops, abbots, etc.), the second estate of nobility (dukes, earls, viscounts, etc.), and the third estate of burgh commissioners (representatives chosen by royal burgh or cities with royal charters). The most powerful member of the first estate was the Archbishop of St. Andrews.

The history of St. Andrews Cathedral dates to the time of the Picts at a place called Cennrigmonaid. The place is believed to be an early name for the site of the Archdiocese of St. Andrews, named after the Apostle Andrew. His relics were said to have been brought to Fife, Scotland by St. Rule from Constantinople sometime in the sixth century. The relics include some of the bones of St. Andrew. According to legend, in 832 CE, the outnumbered Pictish King Óengus mac Fergusa in a battle against the Angles, vowed to make St. Andrew the patron saint of Scotland if he won. On the morning of the battle, clouds formed an *X* shape in the otherwise blue sky, a symbol associated with St. Andrew. Upon his victory, the king followed through with his promise. This legend is the basis for the flag of

Scotland.

The flag of Scotland, a white saltire set against a celestial blue background.
https://commons.wikimedia.org/wiki/File:Flag_of_Scotland.svg

Robert II tried to place his sons into powerful seats with titles and lands. Still, much was out of his control. The powerful families of the Scottish Douglases and Northumberland Percys were at war, culminating in the Battle of Chevy Chase, famously made into an English ballad. This may have been the same battle or related to the Battle of Otterburn in 1388.

In 1390, Robert II died, and his son, Robert III, took his place on the throne. Robert III was believed to have been infirm, suffering from the results of a horse-kicking injury when he was young. He leaned heavily on his younger brother, Robert Stewart, the Duke of Albany. The government stayed in the hands of the duke, who allowed his friend, the Earl of Douglas, to continue raids into England.

Robert III's son, David Stewart, Duke of Rothesay, disappeared, died, or was killed (some suspected by order of the Duke of Albany), so the heir apparent became Robert III's young son James. Robert III had James sent to France to protect him, but the prince was captured by English pirates and became a hostage of Henry IV of England. The shock of this led to Robert III's death. While James remained in England, the Duke of Albany retained control of the government. This led to many noble families expanding their territories, consolidating power, and assembling large private armies.

None of the great Lowland families were as powerful as the Douglases, whose power rivaled the Crown. The founder of the family, James

Douglas, had been a captain of Robert Bruce. His successors were made Lord Warden of the Marches and Lord of Galloway. They then became earls, and through clever marriages, increased the extent of their family connections and possessions to include Galloway, Douglasdale, Annandale, Clydesdale, Lothian, Stirling, and Morayshire. At the beginning of the Stuart dynasty, the fourth Earl of Douglas could muster an army of at least a thousand men.

In the northwest, the self-styled "Kings of the Isles," the MacDonald lords, ruled as autonomous leaders. The lords of Lorne, Argyll, and the Macleans thought of themselves as equals to the Scottish king, not subjects. Over time, the king of the Isles had become allied with the king of England. Eventually, there was a brief power struggle, but the (regent) Duke of Albany was victorious and allied with Henry IV of England.

In 1411, the University of St. Andrews was founded, followed closely by the founding of universities in Glasgow and Aberdeen. This was just the beginning of Scotland's strong tradition of learning.

Two years later, Henry IV died and was succeeded by Henry V, who attacked France and signed the Treaty of Troyes in 1420. This gave him almost half of France and the rest upon the death of the French king. However, the Dauphin, Charles, did not surrender and called upon Scotland to aid him in repelling the English. The Duke of Albany was dead, but his son, John Stewart, Earl of Buchan, brought several Scottish troops who helped turn the tide of the war. Henry V was killed in action, cursing the Scots as he died.

The new regent of Scotland was Murdoch Stewart, the former Duke of Albany's son who had inherited the title. However, James I, who was now twenty-nine and still in England, saw his path clear to claim his throne. In 1424, he returned to his kingdom, sweeping Murdoch aside. However, he did not become the puppet king that England's high council had hoped for. His reign was filled with conflict as the nobles chafed under his more direct rule. He limited the power of the church and commanded that clerics offer prayers to the king and his family.

Walter Stewart, the Earl of Atholl (son of Robert II), had urged the release of James I from England, but for various reasons, had grown to hate the king. Walter's son, David, had been taken as a hostage to England in James' place and had died there. Also, Walter was concerned that the king had designs on his many holdings and titles. He thus conspired with others who opposed the king, including his grandson,

Robert Stewart, the king's chamberlain. They organized an assassination plot and carried it out on February 20, 1437. Though the king was aware of the plot as it was happening and hid from his attackers, he was found and murdered.

However, the assassins had failed to kill the queen and the six-year-old prince, who was now King James II. Walter might have been successful if he had captured the young prince, but the new king was too well protected. Robert Stewart was captured and confessed to his role in the plot. Walter was also quickly captured, along with another main conspirator, Sir Robert Graham. All three were executed. The young King James II was crowned not at Scone but at Holyrood Abbey. Archibald Douglas, 5th Earl of Douglas, became the regent. The king was put into the care of Alexander Livingston of Callendar, keeper of Stirling Castle. The king's mother, Queen Joan, soon married Sir John Stewart, the Black Knight of Lorne.

Archibald Douglas died in 1439, and the 6th Earl of Douglas was William Douglas, Archibald's son. William was invited to the Castle of Edinburgh, where he dined with the ten-year-old king. However, at the end of the dinner, a black bull's head was brought out and set before Douglas. He was soon hurried off and executed. It was known as the "Black Dinner" and was a low point in James' reign, though the young king had nothing to do with the conspiracy that was perpetrated by Sir Alexander Livingston, Lord Chancellor William Crichton, and James Douglas.

When James reached adulthood in 1449, he allied with the Douglas family to remove the Livingstons from the government for their complicity in the murder of William Douglas. However, power struggles between the king and the Douglases led to the murder of another William Douglas— the 8th Earl of Douglas—by the king's own hands. A civil war broke out, which ended with the Crown annexing much of the Douglas lands. The result was that the king no longer faced challenges to his authority from the noble ranks.

King James II was popular and known for mixing with common folk throughout his kingdom. In 1460, while laying siege to Roxburgh Castle, a cannon exploded and killed the king. This left the kingdom to his eight-year-old son, the new King James III. The king's mother, Queen Mary of Guelders, became regent. Mary was an astute ruler but died in 1463. The king was captured by the Boyd family and forced to give them power which they abused.

James III began his personal rule in 1469, and the Boyds and their allies were declared traitors. Some went into exile, while others were captured and executed. By 1476, James had accomplished much in his reign. The Orkney and Shetland islands were officially brought under Scottish dominion, the Boyds had been dealt with, the Archbishop of St. Andrews had been bent to his will, he had concluded a successful treaty with England, and the Lord of the Isles had been greatly reduced in power. He was the undisputed ruler of a kingdom that stretched from the Northern Isles to Berwick-upon-Tweed.

However, many of his actions had made him unpopular. He had angered many nobles by favoring men of low birth and raising them to positions of power. In 1480, the truce with England had broken down following Scottish raids into English territory. In the resulting war, Richard, Duke of Gloucester (the future English King Richard III) launched a full-scale invasion across the Scottish border. However, the English were unsuccessful and retreated to their kingdom. Then, a revolt erupted within Scotland, led by the earls of Angus and Argyll. James III was killed in battle in 1488.

His son and heir was King James IV. The reign of James IV was remarkable, not just because the king was remarkable but because it was a time of peace and prosperity that Scotland had never seen. During his twenty-five years on the throne, James proved to be one of the ablest and most popular of the Stuart kings. He was well-read and excelled at languages, including Gaelic, which was no longer spoken in the Lowlands. He was charming, fun-loving, pious, and forceful. The Scottish people loved him for his open-handedness, friendliness, and his many mistresses and illegitimate children. (This was before the strict ethics of Calvinism had reached Scottish shores.) Literature flourished during his reign, including the epic poem by Blind Harry, *The Wallace*, and William Dunbar's *Thrissil and the Rois* (Thistle and the Rose) Great churches were built. Merchants' homes went from being made of wood to being made of stone. Many castles no longer looked like fortresses but began to look like palaces.

Of course, this was only true in the Lowlands. In the Highlands, life went on much as it had for many centuries. Highlanders were not very interested in the affairs of the king or the pronouncements of Parliament. The Gaelic word *clann* means children, and the chief of the Highland clan was a father, figuratively and sometimes literally, to all the members. He was he the ruler, judge, and protector. He held over them the power of life or death. When he summoned the clansmen to war, they answered at a moment's notice. The clans had their land, their cattle, and each other, and they protected it all with fervor. As the Spanish ambassador observed, "The Scots are not industrious and the people are poor. They spend all their time in wars, and when there is no war they fight one another."[1]

The lords of the Highlands were a rule unto themselves, and their lands were like small kingdoms that were often at odds with each other thanks to feuds and the ever-present need for retribution. They were the MacDonalds and MacLeods of the Western Isles, the northern Mackays, the Mackenzies just south of them, and the great clan of the Campbells at the southern edge of the Highland Line.

James did something no other Stuart king had done: he traveled into the Highlands with a strong, armed escort. He came as a friend, but his entreaties were largely ignored. After all, many of the Highlanders could trace their ancestry back to great kings who were much more admirable than the Anglicized Stuarts. As an old Maclean saying went, "Though poor, I am noble. Thank God that I am a Maclean."[2] James returned, still largely ignored by the Highlanders, and tried a different approach of force. This did not go over any better and led to a flare-up of warfare all along the Highlands. Eventually, James simply settled for placing strong posts in the Highlands and increasing the number of sheriffs and sheriff's courts.

James also greatly increased the power of the Scottish Navy. The most famous addition to the Scottish Navy was the ship *Michael*, or as it was commonly called, *Great Michael*. The ship was too large to be built at any existing Scottish dockyard, so a new dockyard was built at Newhaven. When she was launched in 1511, she was the largest ship afloat, displacing 1,000 tons and featuring twenty-seven large guns. A year later, the English King Henry VIII, not wanting to be outdone, launched the *Henry Grace à Dieu*, which was even larger.

Henry VIII was not just the king of England but also James' brother-in-law. In 1501, the twenty-eight-year-old James had married Henry's sister, Margaret Tudor, who was just twelve years old. The couple would

---

[1] Maclean, Fitzroy, and Magnus Linklater. *Scotland: a concise history.* Thames & Hudson, 2000.

[2] Maclean, Fitzroy, and Magnus Linklater. *Scotland: a concise history.* Thames & Hudson, 2000.

eventually have six children. Two are nameless, and it is assumed they died in infancy. The eldest was James, born in 1507, but he died at one year of age. Next was Arthur, who died at ten months. Then came another James, Duke of Rothesay, born in 1512 and heir apparent. King James also had at least five illegitimate children by four different mothers who were all of noble origins.

James had signed a peace treaty with Henry VIII, but circumstances worked against this peace. England was, once again, at war with France. Scotland and France had enjoyed a long and beneficial alliance, often called the Auld (Old) Alliance, which had derived from their common enemy—the English.

In 1511, the pope created a Holy League against France consisting of the papacy, Spain, Venice, and the Holy Roman Empire. England joined the league, and France, seemingly without an ally, called upon Scotland. James answered the call, and in 1513, he led 40,000 men and a large amount of artillery into England. The English and Scottish forces met in the Battle of Flodden. Led by the Earl of Surrey, the English stopped the advance with a force of 26,000, while the Scottish forces had already diminished to 34,000 due to sickness and desertion. Despite having superior numbers and more modern artillery, the Scottish were defeated, and King James IV was killed in battle. A large number of the highest-ranking nobles in Scotland had also been killed, depleting the country of leadership.

The new king, James V, was barely old enough to walk. His mother, Queen Margaret Tudor, was the sister of the very man who had ordered the death of James IV and had refused to bury him. Henry VIII did this because James IV had been excommunicated by the pope for breaking the treaty with England and staying true to the Auld Alliance. However, after a year or two, things seemed to work themselves out. Henry VIII had not invaded. Queen Margaret had remarried a Scotsman and thus given up her regency. The Duke of Albany, descended from James III and newly arrived from France, was now regent, and the Holy League against France had fallen apart and saved Scotland's old ally.

After being held almost as a captive by the Douglas family, James escaped and began his reign in 1528 at the age of sixteen. He attempted to bring peace and order to the Lowlands and Borderlands and sought to appease the Highlands with varied success. James V married Marie de Guise-Lorraine, a French noblewoman.

In 1534, Henry VIII broke with Rome and created the Church of England. He wanted to impose Protestantism on Scotland as well and invaded in 1542. James retaliated by invading England, but the invasion was half-hearted, and James was soon at odds with his nobles. The king fell ill and was on his deathbed when he received word that his wife had just given birth to a daughter. The king died, and the infant girl, christened Mary, became Mary, Queen of Scots.

Chapter 5: The Reformation and the Rise of Presbyterianism

The Celtic and Pictish gods were long gone and Scotland had been completely Catholic since the beginnings of the kingdom. There had been the Celtic Catholicism of St. Columba, but Roman Catholicism had eventually overcome all. It was not just the dominant but the only religion from the Western Isles to the remaining stones of Hadrian's Wall and the screaming winds of the Orkneys. Yet, in the sixteenth century, something was sweeping across Europe and was now knocking at Scotland's door: the Protestant Reformation.

Martin Luther's *Ninety-five Theses* had been nailed to a church door in 1517. The Swiss theologian, Ulrich Zwingli, had preached on the need to reform the Catholic Church. The French theologian, John Calvin, had published his seminal work *Institutes of the Christian Religion* in 1536. As previously mentioned, Henry VIII embraced the Reformation and Protestantism in his break with the papacy, though not for primarily religious reasons. However, in Scotland in the early 1500s, Roman Catholicism was the only acceptable religious ideology.

There were certainly problems in the Catholic Church in Scotland. Most priests were poor, but there were some glaring exceptions. Parson Adam Colquhoun lived with his mistress, Mary Boyd and their two sons in a Glasgow mansion filled with gold, silver, silk, damask, gilded furniture, feather beds, and a parrot in a cage. The Bishop of Moray provided for all nine of his children from Church funds. According to reports from a cardinal, Scottish nuns were often found surrounded by their children and gave their daughters away with rich dowries taken from church revenues. Fewer people were attending mass, and many churches had fallen into disrepair.

Then, English translations of the Bible began to be smuggled into Scotland. For the first time, Scots could read the "Good Book" themselves. A young nobleman named Patrick Hamilton had come back from the continent a firm Protestant. In 1528, when Archbishop James Beaton arrested him and ordered him to recant, Hamilton refused. The young noble was burned at the stake, slowly, and it was a story of bravery recounted around the kingdom. Still, Protestantism was kept secret in Scotland for many years.

Then, in 1543, a party went to London to consider a treaty in which the English Prince Edward (son of Henry VIII) might marry the infant Mary, Queen of Scots. Accompanying this party was a Scottish scholar named George Wishart, who had earlier fled the country while being investigated for heresy. Wishart soon began to travel as an itinerant preacher, denouncing the errors of the papacy and the corruption of the Church. Along the way, he picked up a disciple by the name of John Knox. In 1546, Wishart was arrested by the orders of Bishop Beaton and then hanged.

John Knox, born near Haddington around 1513, was a firebrand and would have died alongside Wishart if his mentor had not ordered him to fall back. He had been a tutor to two sons of Hugh Douglas and one son of John Cockburn, both Scottish nobles who were reformation-minded, and he returned to this post when Wishart was captured.

Not long after Wishart's execution, Bishop Beaton was murdered by a group in retaliation for Wishart's death. A standoff of sorts then occurred as Reformers held the Castle of St. Andrew's against Catholic forces. Knox took his charges to the relative safety of the castle and was there encouraged to preach. He proved to be an excellent orator and spokesperson for the Reformist movement. The Queen Mother, Mary of Guise, who was regent, requested aid in the situation from her relations in France. Knox soon found himself captured and pressed into rowing in French galleys. After nineteen months in the galley prison, Knox was released and spent five years in England, where he was active in the Reformation.

After spending time in Geneva and Frankfurt, Knox finally returned to Scotland in 1547. He found the country greatly changed. Much of the nobility of Scotland had embraced the Reformation, and he was welcomed in many places and able to preach freely. Still, the bishops of Scotland were intimidated by his presence and called him to trial. When he arrived, he was accompanied by such a great multitude of influential and important persons that the trial was called off.

After a three-year return to Geneva, Knox once again returned to his home in 1559. He was quickly declared an outlaw by the queen regent. As Knox traveled, he preached sermons against the Catholic Church and the Catholic monarch. During many of these sermons, the crowds turned into mobs that ransacked churches and friaries.

Then in 1560, Mary of Guise died amidst an escalating war between Catholic Scots and the French against Protestant Scots and the English. This was ended by the Treaty of Edinburgh. The same year, Knox and five other Protestant ministers convened to write the Scots Confession. Knox and others also began drafting the *Book of Discipline*. These texts created the cornerstones for a new Protestant faith in Scotland known as the Reform Church but often called the Kirk (a Gaelic name meaning "church"). It would eventually be known as the Church of Scotland, or more generally, the Presbyterian Church.

Meanwhile, in 1548, the young Mary, Queen of Scots, had been sent to France, where she was expected to someday wed the Dauphin. The year before, Henry VIII had died, leaving his sickly son Edward as the new king. In 1553, King Edward VI of England died, and his sister, the very Catholic Queen Mary Tudor, took the English throne. Her reign of less than five years was tumultuous, to say the least, and earned her the immortal nickname "Bloody Mary." She died in 1558, the same year that Mary, Queen of Scots, was wed to the Dauphin of France in the Cathedral of Notre Dame in Paris.

It seemed highly likely that France and Scotland would combine into one nation—if not for the fact that France was still Catholic and Scotland was not. It was announced that the crown of England now rested on the head of the young and Protestant Queen Elizabeth I. In 1559, Mary, Queen of Scots' husband, François, succeeded to the throne of France. France soon claimed ownership of England as well because Elizabeth, being Protestant, had no right to the throne while the new French Queen Mary, granddaughter of Henry VII, could claim it. Queen Elizabeth understood the difficult situation she was in and made overtures to the Scottish Protestants—even though Knox was very vocal about his dislike of women rulers.

With Mary of Guise's death in 1560, the Scottish Protestants had won by numbers alone. The country had become Protestant even if the monarchy had not. France withdrew her claims, and the Auld Alliance came to an end. It was the first step in the union with England, and it was not the queens or kings who had made the decision but the common people.

The Kirk was a surprisingly democratic institution for the times. In a Europe that was on the verge of absolute monarchy, the Kirk at least required that ministers be voted upon by the congregation. The congregation also elected the elders, or presbyters (hence the name Presbyterian), and organized care for the poor and sick in their parish. The Kirk also became ingrained in the laws of Scotland. There were very strict rules regarding the Sabbath. For example, a person could be arrested for plucking a chicken on Sunday. There was no dancing, pipe playing, gambling, card playing, or theater acts. One of the most radical ideas of the Kirk was that, while power was given by God, it was not given to monarchs, nobles, or clergy but to the people.

Knox was assisted in much of what he did by George Buchanan, who had studied with John Calvin and Ignatius Loyola, founder of the Jesuits. Buchanan was not just a theologian but a political philosopher, and in his writings, he claimed that political authority was derived from the people. Buchanan wrote this a hundred years before similar ideas were expressed by John Locke, who was a great influence on the Founding Fathers of the United States.

At the end of 1560, after her mother had died and the Treaty of Edinburgh had been signed, Mary, Queen of Scots, was dealt another blow when her husband, the king of France, died as well. The throne of France passed to her young brother-in-law, Charles IX, and Mary returned to Scotland a Catholic monarch in a Protestant nation.

While the Protestants of Scotland welcomed her home with suspicion, the remaining Catholics found their hopes of restoring the Catholic faith in Scotland dashed. John Knox preached against her for hearing mass, dancing, and dressing too elaborately. Mary summoned Knox before her five times, but she was unsuccessful in convincing him to stop speaking out against her. On one occasion, she burst into tears, which clearly moved the minister, but he admitted he would rather endure her tears than betray his commonwealth. Mary attempted to charge him with treason in 1563, but the Privy Council, composed of Catholics and Protestants, dropped the charges against him. In July 1565, Mary married her half-first cousin Henry Stuart, Lord Darnley, in a Catholic ceremony at Holyrood Palace.

Mary was at first in love with Lord Darnley, who is usually described as lackluster, arrogant, and unintelligent, but soon became aware of his lesser qualities. She refused to grant him the Crown Matrimonial, which would make him her successor if she died. Still, Mary became pregnant with her first and only child. Six months into her pregnancy, Lord Darnley became increasingly jealous of her Italian secretary, David Rizzio. In March 1566, Lord Darnley, along with Protestant confederates, stabbed Rizzio fifty-six times, killing him. All the accounts agree that the murder took place in front of the pregnant queen. According to some, Rizzio was the true father of Mary's child, and Darnley's action had been designed to force Mary to give him the Crown Matrimonial. Still, Mary did not acquiesce. On June 19, Mary gave birth to a son named James, the heir to the throne.

Mary and Lord Darnley's marriage continued to struggle. Lord Darnley alienated those who would have support him. He came down with a case of smallpox (though some suggested syphilis), and Mary took him to the Old Provost's lodging at Kirk o' Field, which was a short walk from Holyrood. On the night of February 9, 1567, Mary was attending the wedding of one of her favorite servants while Darnley remained in Kirk o' Field. Around 2 a.m., two explosions rocked the foundations of Kirk o' Field, probably caused by gunpowder barrels placed under Lord Darnley's sleeping quarters. Lord Darnley's dead body and the body of his valet, William Taylor, were found outside the house along with a cloak, dagger, chair, and coat. There were no marks on Lord Darnley's body, so it is believed he was smothered to death. Still, it was clear that Lord Darnley had been murdered. Though it was never proven, James Hepburn, Earl of Bothwell and Lord High Admiral, was heavily implicated.

Eight weeks after Lord Darnley's murder, Mary married James Hepburn, Earl of Bothwell, in a Protestant ceremony. This decision turned both Catholics and Protestants against the queen.

A month later, a group of nobles known as the Confederate Lords gathered an army to rescue Mary from Lord Bothwell, responding to rumors that Lord Bothwell had kidnapped and raped the queen. At

Carberry Hill, the forces of Lord Bothwell met the army of the Confederate Lords, and the queen's supporters were defeated. Lord Bothwell escaped, but the queen surrendered. Mary, only twenty-four years old, was led through the streets of Edinburgh in a short red petticoat amid much derision. On June 1567, she was forced to abdicate the throne in favor of her infant son. That son was crowned King James VI. John Knox delivered a sermon on the occasion and called for Mary's death. Mary's Protestant half-brother, James Stewart, Earl of Moray, was made regent.

Mary was held prisoner at Lochleven Castle near Kinross. She escaped with the assistance of her jailers in 1586 and raised another army but was again defeated, this time by the Earl of Moray. Finally, she crossed the English border in a fishing boat and threw herself at the mercy of England's Queen Elizabeth I. Mary apparently expected Elizabeth to help restore her to the throne of Scotland, but Elizabeth was wary. For one thing, Mary was Catholic while Elizabeth was aligned with the Protestants in Scotland. Secondly, Mary had a claim to the English throne through her grandmother, Margaret Tudor. Elizabeth kept her imprisoned and constantly on the move.

Young King James VI was raised primarily at Stirling Castle, where he was educated to be a member of the Scottish Presbyterian Church. The Protestant nobles of Scotland who had just fought against a Catholic monarch had no interest in repeating history. George Buchanan became the chief of the young king's tutors. He passed on to him regular beatings but also a love of reading and education. In 1570, James' regent, the Earl of Moray, was assassinated by James Hamilton, a supporter of James' mother, Mary. Queen Elizabeth saw the assassination and a corresponding revolt of Catholic nobles in northern England as a sign of Mary's danger. She was kept under close supervision by Elizabeth's chief advisor, William Cecil.

The next regent of Scotland was the Earl of Lennox, James' paternal grandfather. Lennox was killed a year later by supporters of Mary. The Earl of Mar was then made regent, but he, too, died shortly thereafter of a mysterious illness, possibly poisoning. James Douglas, Earl of Morton, became the next regent and remained in that capacity until 1579 when King James was fifteen and declared an adult able to rule on his own. Morton was quickly executed for treason.

After an initial struggle, James consolidated power to himself. One of his chief problems was the role of the Reformed Church in Scotland. He enacted the Black Acts, which brought the Kirk partly under royal control—a decision that would have surely upset James' old tutor George Buchanan had the great thinker not died two years before. The reformist, John Knox, had also died in relative obscurity in 1572. Still, the Presbyterian ministers who followed Knox and Buchanan's *Book of Discipline* felt that the power of the monarchy came from the Kirk. While King James was certainly a Protestant, he was not a Presbyterian. Instead, he felt that the church's power was derived from God's chosen ruler, the king. In this episcopal view, the church was ruled by bishops who were appointed by the monarch—exactly what was done in the Church of England.

In 1584, Mary, Queen of Scots, had agreed to give up any pretensions to the English throne and to retire from public life if only she could be freed from her imprisonment. James at first entertained the idea but then reconsidered and signed an alliance with Elizabeth, abandoning his mother to her fate.

In 1586, Mary was implicated in the Babington Plot to assassinate Queen Elizabeth. She was put on trial for treason, and her defense was spirited. She argued that she had not been able to review the evidence or seek legal counsel and that since she had never been a subject of England, she could not be tried for treason. However, her personal letters made it clear she had approved of the assassination plot, and she was found guilty and sentenced to death. Elizabeth was hesitant to carry out the sentence as she was concerned about setting the precedent of killing a queen. She also feared King James' reaction to the death of his mother. Still, she went through with it, and Mary, Queen of Scots, was beheaded on February 8, 1587.

James made a public declaration of complaint but did nothing to jeopardize his relationship with the English queen. He knew quite well that if Elizabeth died without an heir, which she was almost certain to do, he would have the best claim to the throne of England. In 1603, Queen Elizabeth died, and James was proclaimed king of England later the same day. While this meant that Scotland and England shared a monarch, it did not mean they were united in any other way. They had separate parliaments, laws, courts, and churches, though they did share a similar language. (The Scottish version of English, called "Scots," had been the standard language of the country for centuries. Gaelic was only spoken in a few corners of the kingdom.)

While the two kingdoms were not truly united, James styled himself "King of Great Britain" and forced the Scottish Parliament to use the title, which was used in proclamations and coinage. James moved his court to London and only returned to Scotland once in his long reign.

The change in Scotland was profound. The Scottish people developed an inferiority complex regarding their southern neighbors. No longer were they twin kingdoms on the same island; now England was clearly the favorite sibling. The king preferred England, and Scotland was constantly fending off the invasion of English episcopalian religion, English culture, and English dominance. Scottish nobles flocked to London to work their way into royal affairs. The stereotype of the tight-fisted Scot vying for his share was born.

In 1606, the leader of the Kirk and theological heir of John Knox, Andrew Melville, was imprisoned in the Tower of London by order of the king after speaking out against the popish character of an Anglican service. He was held in the tower for four years. When he was finally freed, he was forced into exile in France, where he remained for the rest of his life.

James introduced more episcopalian elements to the Kirk, and when he died in 1625, the Church of Scotland had a complete assortment of bishops and archbishops. James' son, Charles I, became king of Scotland and England and continued to force episcopalian services and rituals into Scotland. He believed, as his father had, that Presbyterianism was incompatible with the monarchy. The introduction of Charles' *Scottish Prayer Book* in 1637 led to rioting that spread across the kingdom. The rioting, in turn, led to the First Bishops' War in 1639, which only resulted in a few skirmishes, followed by the Second Bishops' War in 1640. The result was a defeat for Charles and a somewhat insignificant truce between him and the Scottish nobles.

Then Charles was forced to deal with a rebellion in Ireland in 1641. Finally, the English Civil War erupted, setting the king against the English Parliament. Charles was eventually captured and, in a surprise move, signed a secret treaty with a faction of Scots. They would invade England and restore the king to his throne on the agreement that Presbyterianism would be impressed on England for three years. The Scots invaded but were defeated by the New Model Army under the command of Oliver Cromwell. Charles was tried, found guilty of treason, and beheaded on January 30, 1649.

While England became a republic, the Scottish Covenanter Parliament agreed to crown Charles' son, Charles II, as the King of Scotland—but only if he agreed to make Presbyterianism the state religion. In 1651, Charles II agreed to the Covenanter Parliament's demands and was crowned king. His abandonment of episcopalian religion was unpopular in England and led to a war in which Cromwell defeated a Scottish force yet again. Charles II led an invasion force into England but (like his father) was defeated, though he managed to escape to Normandy. Cromwell then put the British Isles under military rule, which ended when Cromwell died in 1658. Charles II was invited back to England and crowned in 1661.

Once again, the king of Scotland, Ireland, and England was the same man, and England became the focal point of the monarch's attention. However, it was not just tradition but economics that played a role in England's status. The southern British kingdom now had colonies around the globe and a burgeoning global empire.

Scottish immigration to the English American colonies had begun in 1650 when Cromwell had sent defeated Scots to Maine, Massachusetts, and New Hampshire. Voluntary Scottish immigration soon followed, especially to the Carolinas and New Jersey. Yet, long before this, in 1629, the Scottish had founded the colony of Nova Scotia. However, this colony was soon abandoned and handed over to the French after the Treaty of Suza.

The most well-known and disastrous of Scotland's colonial attempts was the settlement of New Caledonia on the shore of the isthmus of Panama in 1698. It was called the Darien scheme after the colony's location—the Gulf of Darien.

The Wars of the Three Kingdoms that preceded the restoration of Charles II had been hard on Scotland, but so were the "Seven Ill Years" in the 1690s, which brought widespread crop failure and a huge loss of life. As a result of these hard times, the Scottish Parliament enacted wide-sweeping programs to improve the lives of the Scottish people. The Bank of Scotland, based on the very successful Bank of England, was formed. The Act of Settling Schools was passed, which created a school in every parish in the country. This radical legislation would have far-reaching consequences: a generation later, the Scottish people were widely regarded as the most well-read and educated people in Western Europe.

Parliament also created the Company of Scotland, which it hoped to rival the great colonial companies of Africa, Asia, and the West Indies.

However, the East India Company saw this as a direct threat. As a result, the Company of Scotland found it all but impossible to raise funds from English or Dutch investors. The new king, William II (and III of England), gave only mild support to the cause because he did not want to upset the Spanish, who claimed all of Panama for themselves. Consequently, the Scottish people, both noble and common, provided all the funds for the expedition, which amounted to £400,000 sterling— roughly one-fifth of all the wealth in the country.

Five ships sailed from Leith in July 1698 and landed near the mouth of the Darien River in November. The expedition consisted of 1,200 people, many of them former soldiers. They built a fort and a watchtower and then constructed a group of huts they called "New Edinburgh." Growing crops proved difficult, the natives were unwilling to trade, and disease began to run rampant through the colony. The few trading vessels that stopped were not interested in the trinkets the Scots had brought with them. To avoid angering the Spanish, King William instructed the English and Dutch not to provide supplies to the Scots.

After just eight months, the colony was abandoned. Only 300 of the original 1,200 survived, and two ships limped into New York harbor. The only colonists who made it home were considered a disgrace and disowned by their families. However, the fate of the colony did not reach Scotland in time to stop another 1,000 brave souls headed to Panama. This group rebuilt and took the offensive against the Spanish, but this only led to the Spanish besieging the settlers' fort until they surrendered. It was the last attempt at a Scottish colony.

Then in 1702, William II died and was succeeded by his sister-in-law, Anne. Queen Anne had been the sister of William's wife, Queen Mary, and the daughter of the unpopular James II. In her first speech to Parliament, trying to distance herself from her Dutch brother-in-law, she said, "As I know my heart to be entirely English, I can very sincerely assure you there is not anything you can expect or desire from me which I shall not be ready to do for the happiness and prosperity of England."[3] This must have come as a bitter pill to her Scottish subjects. Yet, Scotland was in no state to argue. The Darien scheme had wrecked the economy, and famine and cold had decimated the population. It was five years later that Queen Anne proposed a union between the two kingdoms of Britain.

---

[3] Maclean, Fitzroy, and Magnus Linklater. *Scotland: a concise history.* Thames & Hudson, 2000.

Chapter 6: Union with England— The 1707 Act of Union and Its Consequences

King William III of England, also known as William of Orange.

It was a long and winding road that led to the 1707 Act of Union that dissolved the Scottish and English governments to create a new British government. Of course, the relationship between the two countries had long been fraught with tension and occasionally escalated to outright bloodshed, as a review of these events will show.

As we mentioned, the ascendancy of the Scottish King James VI to the throne of England as James I did not suddenly unite the kingdoms but instead did quite the reverse. The Scots felt ignored at best and oppressed at worst. James did all he could to turn the Scots into Englishmen. James' son, Charles, had been born in Scotland but left for England when he was three in 1603. He did not return until 1633 after he had been king for eight years. He had no understanding of Scotland and was a devout episcopalian with a strong dislike of democratic assemblies. In 1629, he demanded that the religious practices of Scotland should conform to the Church of England. When he finally bothered to come to Scotland to be crowned, it was done with full Anglican rites.

By 1638, Charles had only made matters worse. Representatives from the nobles, gentry, burghs, and clergy met to sign a document called the National Covenant, which opposed Charles' demands but did not call for revolution. Soon, the document was copied and distributed throughout the country, and many more signed. From this came the cascading events that led to the Bishops' Wars and eventually the English Civil War.

The Scots were in a good position during the war. The Covenanters (those who followed the National Covenant) signed the Solemn League and Covenant with the English Parliament to do just the thing they hated Charles for—namely, forcing their religion onto the English. But this was undone by another Scot and a former Covenanter, James Graham the 1st Marquess of Montrose (known as the Great Montrose), who rose in support of King Charles. With an army of Irish and Highlanders, he began crushing larger armies and sacking important cities throughout Scotland. Montrose was eventually defeated, but his actions undermined the Covenanters' power, which had shifted to Oliver Cromwell and his army. Cromwell had no interest in dealing with the Covenanters or seeing Presbyterianism in England.

The Scots then handed over Charles but almost instantly questioned this decision. They began plotting with the imprisoned king to bring him back to the throne and impose Presbyterianism on England. This, of course, failed to happen, and when the news reached Scotland that

Charles had been executed, the universal response was shock. No matter how much the Covenanters opposed Charles, they never imagined he might be killed.

The Great Montrose's chief opponent and the primary power among the Covenanters, Archibald Campbell, the 1st Marquess of Argyll, immediately contacted Charles I's son, also Charles, and proclaimed him king in Edinburgh. After initial failures and the eventual death of Cromwell, Charles II was on the throne of England and administered Scotland, like his father and grandfather before him, through a Privy Council. Despite the support of people like Argyll, Charles II soon undid all the measures enacted by the Covenanters. Many openly defied him, and violent outbursts ensued.

Charles II died in 1685 and was succeeded by his brother James VII and II, the Duke of York, who had been born in the Church of England but converted to Catholicism while in France. Archibald Campbell organized a rebellion against the new king. This was encouraged by James' Dutch son-in-law, William of Orange. However, the rebellion was a failure, and Campbell was executed.

James' policies were increasingly unpopular. When his second (Catholic) wife gave birth to a son, thus confirming the likelihood of a new Catholic dynasty in both countries, a group of nobles invited William of Orange and his wife, Mary the daughter of James, to come to Britain with an army. In 1689, William and Mary landed in England. James soon fled, and the Protestant couple were crowned king and queen. The Glorious Revolution was complete.

There were some, especially in the Highlands, who remained true to King James VII. These formed the first group to be called Jacobites. William sent an army to defeat a Jacobite army in Perthshire, but his army, led by General James Mackay, was annihilated. However, the Highlanders soon faded back into their homes in the mountains and glens.

William decided to set an example and demanded an oath of fealty from the clan heads by January 1, 1692. A rebellion was avoided when the exiled James sent word that the Highlanders should comply. Only two did not meet the deadline. One was the leader of the powerful MacDonells of Glengarry, and the other was MacIain, the chieftain of a minor sept (branch) of Clan Donald, the MacDonalds of Glencoe. MacIain arrived to take the oath on January 6, unable to make the journey to the proposed location due to inclement weather. The MacDonell leader was forgiven, but MacIain became William's example.

A group of Robert Campbell's troops arrived as guests in Glencoe. They spent weeks drinking and playing cards until they received the orders to put the entire sept to the sword. On February 13, early in the morning, the troops systematically slaughtered the MacDonalds as they slept and burned their cottages to the ground. William succeeded in putting a temporary halt to Jacobinism in the Highlands, but Scotland grew to distrust their new monarch.

It was not until the Darien scheme (detailed in the last chapter) that many Scots began to see the only way of saving their country from ruin was through union with England. In 1702, Queen Anne (William's sister-in-law) came to the throne, but she had no heir. The English were concerned about another Stuart restoration as James VII and II's son, James Edward, was alive and still a Roman Catholic. So, the English signed the 1701 Act, establishing that the throne would pass through Sophia, the Electress of Hanover, a German princess and the granddaughter of James VI and I.

However, the English were also concerned that the Stuarts might come through the "back door," meaning the throne of Scotland. The Scots, aware of the situation, passed the Act of Security. This said the successor to the Scottish throne would be a Protestant descendant from the House of Stuart—but not the same monarch as in England unless Scotland was given equal trading rights and freedom of government and religion. The English were incensed by this bold move, and tensions rose. The queen could not afford a war with Scotland since she was already at war with France. In 1705, she sent the young Duke of Argyll, the Lord High Commissioner, to persuade the Scottish Parliament to authorize negotiations for a Treaty of Union.

So on October 3, 1707, the Scottish Parliament met in Edinburgh to vote on the Treaty of Union. The treaty had been negotiated by two teams of commissioners, one Scottish and one English, but there was little to negotiate as both parties were handpicked by Queen Anne and devised the treaty exactly according to her specifications.

Quite simply, the Crown wanted the incorporation of Scotland into England. The treaty created the Kingdom of Great Britain, governed by one monarch and one Parliament. The seat of government would be in London. The Scottish Privy Council would lose all its power, while

England assumed control over taxes, customs, and excise duties for both nations as well as over military and foreign affairs. The Scottish Parliament would dissolve, and in its place, the Scottish would have forty-five seats out of 558 in the new British Parliament. Only sixteen Scottish nobles would be allowed into the House of Peers.

The appointed head of the pro-union forces in Parliament was James Douglas, Marquis of Queensbury. London had given him 20,000 pounds to buy the votes if needed. Ultimately, he didn't need the whole amount and pocketed 12,000 pounds for his troubles. The Scottish nobility had fallen on hard times, and the promise of access to the English trade routes that encircled the globe was something they couldn't reject on any grounds.

The spokesperson for the motley collection of anti-unionists was one of the founders of the Darien scheme, Andrew Fletcher of Saltoun. Fletcher was an enigmatic figure. In 1685, he had joined the Earl of Argyll in opposing James VII and II's succession but was sent abroad for murdering Argyll's chief guide. In exile, Fletcher became friends with William of Orange but turned against him after the Glorious Revolution, realizing that William wasn't going to set Scotland free. For all his supposed love of freedom, Fletcher once proposed turning the entirety of the Scottish peasantry into slaves.

In the Parliament's consideration of the Treaty of Union, there were twenty-five articles to consider separately. First and foremost was the ability of Scottish merchants to enter English overseas markets. The pro-union side argued that, while it sounded like Scotland was giving up political autonomy, this was an illusion. London had been administering Scottish affairs for over a century. If the Parliament dissolved, the only people who'd notice were the members themselves.

Still, the anti-union party, or at least a portion of it, was more concerned with the future of Scotland's religion. The treaty said nothing about the Kirk, and Presbyterian ministers widely opposed the treaty for fear that England would use its power to dismantle the church. Then, at the last moment, the General Assembly of the Kirk of Scotland gave its consent to the treaty. The assembly had been won over by the efforts of William Carstares, principal of the University of Edinburgh and moderator of the General Assembly.

Finally, on November 4, Parliament voted in favor of the first article—the creation of Great Britain. The next two articles passed, as well. Article

4, which concerned the freedom of trade, was next on the docket. This was when Fletcher rose to make his rebuttal to the chief reason pro-unionists supported the treaty. In an eloquent speech, he explained that while England might prosper from trade, Scotland never could. It was not in the nature of the Scottish to be merchants. His speech fell on deaf ears, and the article passed with 156 votes for and 19 against.

Over the next two months, Parliament made its way through the rest of the articles with little opposition. Then came Article 22, which abolished the Scottish Parliament. The debate began with John Dalrymple, 1st Earl of Stair. Dalrymple was a man without sympathy who had been largely responsible for the massacre at Glencoe. He called the people killed, including women and children, a "sept of thieves." Dalrymple explained that the limited number of seats for Scotland in the new Parliament made absolute sense. The English, collectively, would be paying thirty-five times more in taxes than the Scots. So, their numbers in Parliament should reflect that. Really, Dalrymple argued, Scotland was getting the better of the deal at ten-to-one representation.

Article 22 passed by forty votes. Dalrymple left the chambers, exhausted, and returned to his Edinburgh lodgings, where he went to sleep and never woke up. He was declared a martyr to the cause of union.

Not long after, Parliament voted in favor of the rest of the articles and then on the whole treaty. The Kingdom of Scotland thus ceased to exist. "Now there's an end to an old song," remarked Lord Seafield.[4] Due to the angry mob in Edinburgh that opposed the treaty, the members had to sign the final documents secretly and then promptly flee to London.

Part of the treaty involved compensation for investors who had lost so much in the Darien scheme. Many were rewarded for their pro-union votes—but perhaps not as much as they hoped. The Marquis of Queensberry benefited the most, of course, and was awarded an earldom by the queen and a year stipend.

In the short term, it seemed that those opposed to the treaty were right. The English made it clear that Scotland was subservient to England, and despite promises otherwise, Presbyterians were not secure. Scotland was once again being primed for revolution.

---

[4] Maclean, Fitzroy, and Magnus Linklater. *Scotland: a concise history.* Thames & Hudson, 2000.

Chapter 7: Jacobite Risings

The general unrest in Scotland over the union encouraged the Jacobites, who hoped for the return of James Francis Edward (James VII and II's son) and the Stuart dynasty, to push toward their goal. When Queen Anne fell ill in 1714, a Jacobite coup seemed possible. When Anne subsequently died, Parliament acted quickly and proclaimed her German cousin, son of the Electress Sophia, King George I of the House of Hanover. The new monarch was generally disagreeable to his subjects. He was unattractive physically and personally to the British people, and (early in his reign, at least) he did not even speak English. Though he was Protestant, he was neither Anglican nor Presbyterian but Lutheran.

Two political factions grew during this time. Whigs typically supported King George and the nobility, while Tories drew support from the landed gentry. Many opposed George in favor of the Catholic James Francis Edward Stuart.

John Erskine, the 6th Earl of Mar, had originally favored the union even though he would be forced to surrender his position as the Secretary of State of Scotland. He had hoped he could secure a lucrative position in George's government, but the king completely ignored him. Lord Mar left London in haste. In 1715, he called on his friends and dependents to join him in a traditional stag hunt. After the hunt, while drinking honeyed whiskey, Lord Mar told those gathered that he now regretted his support for the "cursed union" and pledged to undo it and return Scotland to her ancient liberties.

According to some sources, Lord Mar, known as "Bobbing John" to his contemporaries due to his frequent changes in loyalty, had received a letter from James Edward directing him to take this action. Other sources claim James was ignorant of the plot until after Mar had proclaimed him king.

When Lord Mar raised the Scottish standard at Castletown in Braemar, the ornamental ball on top of the flagpole fell off and struck the ground. This caused a murmur among the more superstitious present, but Lord Mar took no notice. He quickly raised an army of 12,000 clansmen, who all declared for King James in a rising called "the Fifteen" for the year in which it took place, 1715.

The rising had a good start, and Lord Mar soon captured Perth. All that stood in his way to the English border was 2,000 soldiers under the command of John Campbell, 2nd Duke of Argyll. However, Lord Mar might have been an excellent politician, but he was not a military leader. He stayed in Perth for several weeks, missing the opportunity for decisive action. He sent his best commander, Mackintosh of Borlum, with 2,000 troops to meet with Jacobites on both sides of the Scottish and English border.

Old Borlum, as he was known, took it upon himself to move toward Edinburgh, but he was headed off by the experienced Duke of Argyll. After turning south and combining forces with William Gordon, 6th Viscount of Kenmure, and Thomas Forster, an English Jacobite, the army met the Duke of Argyll in the Battle of Preston. Under the command of Forster, the Jacobite army was defeated, and Forster offered his surrender. Many Jacobites were captured, and some were executed—including the Viscount of Kenmure. Both Borlum and Forster were captured but managed to escape.

Meanwhile, Simon Fraser, 11th Lord Lovat (the contested Chief of Clan Fraser), had returned to raise his clan. Fraser was known as "the Fox" and, by that time, had double dealings, death sentences, a forced marriage, and imprisonment in his past. His claim as Lord of Lovat had been in doubt when Alexander Mackenzie had married the heiress to the title and moved into the Lovat home of Beaufort Castle. Yet, Simon still commanded the allegiance of many of the Frasers who did not recognize Mackenzie's leadership.

Fraser had been imprisoned in France but was then allowed to go to London, where he was living when the 1715 uprising broke out. He asked the Crown to be allowed to go home and raise his clan. He was given permission, but knowing the history of "the Fox," the English questioned his motives. Fraser erased all doubt when he led his clan to seize Inverness Castle on behalf of King George. The Frasers that had joined Lord Mar defected, as did many of the Gordons. For his trouble, Simon was given a full pardon and restored to his position as Lord of Lovat, once again able to collect the income associated with it. Andrew Mackenzie, who had joined the Jacobite cause, was captured and thrown in jail. The Whig clans of the north soon controlled the whole region.

Lord Mar once again advanced on the Duke of Argyll, and the armies met at Sheriffmuir. Lord Mar's right routed the duke's left, while the duke's right did the same to Lord Mar's left. The Duke of Argyll suffered more losses than Lord Mar, but Lord Mar had once again failed to push his advantage, and this allowed the Duke of Argyll to retreat. The battle was indecisive, but in a wider sense, it was a great loss for the Jacobites. The Duke of Argyll still held Stirling and still blocked Lord Mar's progress to England. Lord Mar continued to wallow in Perth, losing large numbers of soldiers daily as the Highlanders again faded into their mountains and glens.

Perhaps the most startling thing to consider is that the fall of Inverness Castle at the Battle of Preston and the indecisive Battle of Sheriffmuir happened on roughly the same day— November 13, 1715. Once the news reached Lord Mar, it became apparent that the uprising had lost, and the Jacobite cause would need to be deferred. Still, Lord Mar remained in Perth.

Then, in December 1715, James Francis Edward Stuart, known to his enemies as James the Pretender, landed at Peterhead just north of Aberdeen. The cause to restore the Stuarts to the throne was already lost. He took the situation in his typical melancholy fashion. "For me it is no new thing to be unfortunate," he said to those gathered, "since my whole life from my cradle has been a constant series of misfortunes."[5] Lord Mar soon abandoned Perth. Once he reached Montrose, he and James took a ship to France. James left a message for the Jacobite Highlanders, who remained to save themselves.

The British government then set about restoring peace to Scotland. Many rebels were taken prisoner and executed. However, in 1717, the

---

[5] Maclean, Fitzroy, and Magnus Linklater. *Scotland: a concise history.* Thames & Hudson, 2000.

Indemnity Act, also called the Act of Grace and Free Pardon, freed most of the prisoners and allowed them to settle at home or overseas. However, there were exceptions, most notably the entire Clan Gregor, who were mostly known as outlaws. This included the famous Rob Roy Macgregor, who had joined the 1715 Jacobite Rising and afterward terrorized the Highlands as an outlaw who waged war on James Graham, the 1st Duke of Montrose. He was immortalized in Sir Walter Scott's novel *Rob Roy*, which deals with the time of the Fifteen. John Erskine's title, the Earl of Mar (which was made a dukedom by James the Pretender), was forfeited and remained vacant for over a century.

When James Francis Edward left Scotland, many of the Scottish people had little reason to love him; on his return to France, he was not welcome either. His patron, French King Louis XIV, had died, and France had aligned with the House of Hanover. James finally settled in the Italian walled city of Urbino and then in Rome as a guest of Pope Innocent XIII. There, he created a Stuart court in exile and lived in splendor, though he still dealt with waves of melancholy. In 1719, he married a Polish princess, and together they had two sons: Charles Edward and Henry Benedict.

Then, in 1719, the Jacobites found they had a very powerful ally in Cardinal Giulio Alberoni, a powerful statesman in the Spanish court under Philip V. Alberoni probably didn't care whether a Stuart or Hanover occupied the throne of Scotland, but he was interested in distracting England, which had joined the Quadruple Alliance against Spain.

Alberoni sent William Mackenzie, the 5th Earl of Seaforth, and George Keith, 10th Earl Marischal, who were in exile after participating in the rising of 1715, to begin a new rising in the Highlands. Accompanying them were two frigates and 300 Spanish soldiers. He would also send twenty-seven ships and 5,000 troops directly to England. The larger party was scattered by storms and never made it. In fact, there has been some speculation that Alberoni never intended for that landing to go through.

The Scottish party landed and marched to Glenshiel, where they were met by superior government forces. They were soon defeated. The Spanish surrendered, and the Scots dispersed into the hills. Earl Marischal returned to exile with James the Pretender, who made him part of his Order of the Garter. He soon found service within the government of Prussia. Seaforth would later be pardoned by George II.

The British government continued with measures to pacify the Highlands. In 1720, efforts were made to stamp out the Gaelic language, and in 1725, Highlanders were banned from carrying arms in public. Under General Wade, a program of road building began to penetrate the most important regions and connect them to Fort William, Fort Augustus, and Fort George. Several Independent Highland Companies were recruited by Whig leaders and formed a regiment called the Black Watch, which performed police duties.

In 1727, George I was succeeded by his son, George II. England's attitude toward Scotland remained much the same. Taxes became a perpetual point of contention, especially on malt (an ingredient in whiskey) and salt, which led to riots. Smuggling became common, and smugglers were popular heroes. The House of Hanover reacted with harsh punishment, which did nothing to endear them to their Scottish subjects.

England was again at war with Spain in 1739, followed the next year by war with France. The Jacobites saw an opportunity in Prince Charles Edward Stuart, a young man of energy, courage, and charisma. In January 1744, Bonnie Prince Charlie, as he would be called, left his father in Rome and headed to France. His hope of being recognized as heir to the throne of England, Scotland, and Ireland by Louis XV went unfulfilled. Even many of the Jacobites in Scotland seemed reluctant to support him.

So, after he sold some of his mother's jewelry, Prince Charles outfitted a frigate and a ship of the line and set sail for Scotland. The ship, *Elizabeth*, turned back, but the frigate, *Doutelle*, landed on the island of Eriskay in the Outer Hebrides. The nobles there refused to see Charles, and one told him to go home. "I am come home," he replied[6].

Prince Charles then went to Moidat, where Clan MacDonald of Clanranald rallied to his cause. An army of 900 was raised, and Charles' father, James, was once again proclaimed king. The prince gathered 3,000 clansmen and marched on Edinburgh, which he captured. He then defeated government forces at Prestonpans. But he lingered in Edinburgh for more than a month.

George II recalled Dutch and English troops from Flanders, while Prince Charles hoped for support from France. The French sent supplies and money, but no troops. In November, he crossed the border and

---

[6] Maclean, Fitzroy, and Magnus Linklater. *Scotland: a concise history.* Thames & Hudson, 2000.

headed toward London. He hoped to be joined by English Jacobites, but this did not happen. Charles' position was advanced on by three separate armies: General Wade from the northeast, the Duke of Chamberlain through the Midlands, and another from the capital. In all, Charles was surrounded by some 30,000 troops to his roughly 5,000 clansmen.

Charles' council advised him to retreat, which he finally agreed to. He had an indecisive battle at Falkirk and then met the Duke of Cumberland's army at the Battle of Culloden. The prince's army was exhausted, hungry, and ill-prepared while Cumberland, who was the son of George II and also a prince, had an army that was well-trained, well-rested, and well-fed. Charles' army was crushed at every point. Bonnie Prince Charlie watched with tears as his hopes of a Stuart restoration were washed away in blood.

The Battle of Culloden would be called the Forty-five Rebellion or simply the Forty-Five, and it was the last serious attempt to put James Edward Stuart on the throne of Scotland or England. After the defeat at Culloden, one of Charles' generals, Lord George Murray, Duke of Atholl, organized a retreat to Ruthven Barracks to continue the fight, but Prince Charles told the army to disperse. Lord Murray left for France, hoping to return.

The Scots who had joined this last revolt felt understandably ill-used. They had risked their lives and titles on promises from exiled Scots with little to lose and Bonnie Prince Charlie's promises of English and French support that never materialized. Lord Murray, like many of the Jacobite nobles, went into exile and petitioned James Stuart in Rome, where he received a pension.

Lord Murray's younger brother, James, however, had been part of Lord Cumberland's army at Culloden. James Murray became the 2nd Duke of Atholl since both of his older brothers had joined the 1719 and 1745 Jacobite rebellions. James, unlike his brothers, was loyal to the House of Hanover, and his loyalty was rewarded. He was made Lord Privy Seal and invested with the Order of the Thistle. He gained the baronage of Strange and sovereignty of the Isle of Man. Thus, he was both a Scottish peer and an English baron. He sat in the British Parliament with much prestige. James was succeeded as Duke of Atholl by his brother George's son, John Murray. John was married to James Murray's daughter, Charlotte (his first cousin), who inherited the rest of her father's titles.

After the Battle of Culloden, Prince Charles fled first to Gorthleck and then to Invergarry Castle. He was aware that government forces were hunting for him and fled again, always one step ahead of his pursuers. Highlanders aided him in his flight, promising not to tell anyone of his whereabouts. He then made for The Hebrides, going secretly from island to island. Flora MacDonald, a minor noble who was not known to support the Jacobite cause, helped him sail to the Isle of Skye. Charles was disguised as an Irish maid named "Betty Burke." MacDonald was arrested for her part in the ruse and was held in the Tower of London. She was eventually freed under the Act of Indemnity of 1747.

Charles returned to mainland Scotland and eventually took a ship to France. King Louis XV welcomed him warmly but was not forthcoming with any aid to the cause of the Stuart restoration. Charles soon fell out with his brother Henry, who had joined the Catholic Church as a cardinal, and his father, James. Charles later went so far as to renounce his Catholic faith to gain support from the Protestants in Scotland and England, but it did not help.

In 1766, James, the Old Pretender, died. Pope Clement XIII had recognized James as the rightful king of Scotland, England, and Ireland but did not extend this same recognition to Charles, his heir. Charles could not gather any support for his cause and, in his later years, fell into drunkenness. He referred to himself as the "Duke of Albany" and in his will passed on this title to his illegitimate daughter, Charlotte. He died of a stroke in 1788.

Three Scottish lords were beheaded after the Forty-five, but most of those involved were pardoned. The military road system was completed by the government, and more forts were added in the Highlands. The clan system was further weakened with additional political measures. The most significant was the Heritable Jurisdictions (Scotland) Act of 1746, which ended the feudal power of chiefs over clansmen. Highland dress was outlawed, though this restriction was later repealed.

The Jacobite movement did not completely end after 1745, but it ceased to be a major consideration for the government. Never again would a large army threaten to restore the Stuart dynasty by force. The Duke of Cumberland, soon after his victory at Culloden, resigned from the military and died of a stroke in 1765.

Debate about the exact motives of the last Jacobite rebellion continues. Certainly, various people joined the cause for various reasons. Prince

Charles, despite his image of being courageous and charming, was not quite the leader the Jacobites had hoped for. Many joined the cause not because they opposed the House of Hanover but because they opposed the union and hoped for a free Scottish kingdom or even republic. Scottish exiles had joined Charles because he offered the opportunity to not just win back the titles and land they had lost but to gain more in the process.

All of these were a threat to the established government in London, and many Scots declined to involve themselves in Jacobite risings. Continuous warfare had drained them in many ways, and the new unified British government was not just as good as any government they had had before. In many ways, it was better, and it continued to get better as the union progressed.

Chapter 8: The Scottish Enlightenment

Scottish philosopher David Hume.
https://commons.wikimedia.org/wiki/File:David_Hume_Ramsay.jpg

The Scottish Enlightenment started to pick up just as the dust was settling from the Jacobite risings of 1715 and 1719. It continued through the Forty-Five and into the nineteenth century. Many of the writers, scientists, philosophers, and teachers of the Scottish Enlightenment could also be found in armed militia protecting the cities from the army of Bonnie Prince Charlie. They were all Whigs and supporters of the House of Hanover and the new British government.

The English began thinking of Scotland as a newly acquired province, but the great minds of the Enlightenment showed them that Scotland could rival and overcome them in areas where only the "gentleman" was allowed. The Scottish might have had rough accents and might have stood openmouthed before the sprawling metropolis of London, but they could also be brilliant. Their fierce tongues and wit could drive them to amazing feats of intelligence.

When the Scottish writer James Boswell met the English writer Samuel Johnson, Boswell apologized for being Scottish. and Johnson accepted that it was something many Scottish people were sorry for. Still, Johnson took Boswell under his wing because he saw something in the young man from Edinburgh; this would be revealed in Boswell's ground-breaking biography of Johnson. Scotland, like that young man, was being offered an opportunity that would help the nation see its potential.

The national circumstances in the decades following the Act of Union were transformative for the people of Scotland. They were the junior partner in the relationship, but this position afforded them much personal freedom. Aside from subduing the diminishing threat of Jacobinism, England left Scotland largely to her own devices. The Scots enjoyed a strong government that didn't bother to interfere as long as order remained.

The short-term trade-offs of the union turned into long-term benefits. In the 1720s, grain exports doubled. The greatest problem of Lowland farmers was not famine but surplus. Glasgow merchants began trading with the American colonies and were running the lucrative tobacco trade by the mid-1700s. William Mackintosh of Borlum, the Jacobite leader imprisoned in Edinburgh Castle, observed in 1729 that the middle class was better dressed, furnished, and housed than they'd ever been. It was this, perhaps more than anything else, that doomed the risings of 1715 and 1745. Middle-class Scotland had no good reason to overthrow the English yoke. They were too busy gaining wealth and increasing their standard of living.

It was in this changing world that several important thinkers emerged. One was Francis Hutcheson, a soft-spoken clergyman and teacher.

Another was Henry Home, Lord Kames, a rough-and-tumble lawyer and judge. Separately, they would spawn the Scottish Enlightenment and inspire a generation to a new understanding of humanity. The great books of Scotland and the Enlightenment in general include Hutcheson's *System of Moral Philosophy* and Kames' *Sketches of the History of Man*. From these works came the works of David Hume, Adam Smith, William Robertson, Adam Ferguson, and Thomas Reid—what we today call the social sciences. Among so many things, the Scottish Enlightenment produced the *Encyclopedia Britannica*, which was first published in Edinburgh in 1768. And, from the name of that encyclopedia, we can see the mindset of this new generation: they were British above all else.

Francis Hutcheson

Francis Hutcheson was born in Northern Ireland, an Ulster Scot or what we today would call Scots-Irish, but he was thoroughly Scottish in upbringing, religion, and outlook. After attending the University of Glasgow, he went to Dublin in 1718 and there joined a circle of intellects surrounding Robert (Viscount) Molesworth. From them, he absorbed the works of English luminaries John Locke, Isaac Newton, Samuel Clarke, Jonathan Swift, and Anthony Ashley Cooper, 3rd Earl of Shaftesbury.

Hutcheson developed a concept of humanity far removed from the fire and brimstone of John Knox and the Kirk, though still rooted in Christianity. He believed that everyone is born with a sense of right and wrong. Moral reasoning is expressed through our emotions, and the most important of these is love, particularly love for others. Everyone's goal is happiness, which is obtained by making others happy. In 1725, Hutcheson published his first book, *An Inquiry into the Original of Our Ideas of Beauty and Virtue*. It was an instant success.

Hutcheson found a patron in Archibald Campbell (Lord Ilay), whose father had beaten the Earl of Mar at Sheriffmuir and was a staunch Whig. With Ilay's help, Hutcheson was placed at the University of Glasgow in the Chair of Moral Philosophy. There, Hutcheson influenced a generation of thinkers, including a young student named Adam Smith, who came to Glasgow in 1737.

Hutcheson explained that the crucial element to allowing the good nature of humanity to spread was liberty. Human beings, he explained, are born free and equal. These are "right" and universal, meaning they should be enjoyed by everyone regardless of social position or even gender. The worst crime against these rights was slavery, which Hutcheson greatly opposed. He died in 1746 as Bonnie Prince Charlie was fleeing to the continent.

Henry Home, Lord Kames

Henry Home was the son of a gentleman from Kames, in Berwickshire. He was raised Episcopalian and became an advocate (lawyer) and a member of the Scottish Bar in 1723. In 1737, Lord Kames found a position as curator of the Advocates Library and turned the institution into a repository for books on many subjects that helped spawn the Enlightenment in Edinburgh. When he became a judge in 1752, he chose the title Lord Kames, derived from the name of his family home.

Lord Kames surrounded himself with bright young academics, including John Miller, Adam Smith, James Boswell, and David Hume. Hume was particularly close to Lord Kames, who was like a father figure to the young philosopher. Yet, like father and son, they often quarreled, especially concerning faith.

Lord Kames' contribution to Enlightenment thinking was mainly in the realm of history. He was also a founding member of the Philosophical Society of Edinburgh. Kames, being a judge, was particularly interested in the reason for laws and government. He proposed that human communities progressed through four distinct stages based largely on the way they obtained and kept their property. First came hunting and fishing, then herding (which led to animal domestication), and then agriculture, which occasioned the creation of laws to protect that individual property. Lastly came commercial society, where men bought and sold goods. This required even more complicated systems of laws concerning contracts and loans. Commerce, like Hutcheson's liberty, led to more human interactions. These interactions refined and polished the manners of humanity, leading to a more sophisticated "gentleman" who would be likely to express the selflessness within his heart. Commercial society was also known as *capitalism*, and this was the only stage at which Kames thought Hutcheson's natural altruism could thrive.

Kames' four-stage theory of societies was at once liberating and oppressive. It caused the modern mind to see change not as something terrifying but as something beneficial to the natural progress of society. However, his theory also helped feed racial stereotypes about the "savage" and "uncivilized" societies that were not commercial, according to this Scottish model. Kame continued to write and work as a judge for the rest of his life. He died naturally at the age of eighty-seven.

James Boswell

Boswell grew up in Edinburgh, the son of the judge Lord Auchinleck. He was mentored by Lord Kames, who encouraged his intellectual and literary interests. He left his home city and arrived in London in 1760 at age twenty. There he found that his greatest hindrance to success was his native land. The new King George III had selected a Scotsman, Lord Bute, as prime minister, and Bute turned out to be very unpopular. It was not a good time to be a Scot or to speak not only with an accent but in a very different form of Anglo-Saxon English (then called Scots). Self-conscious Scottish noblemen and ladies attended lectures and took classes to speak more like the English.

However, Boswell's first trip to London was an escape from the University of Glasgow, where he was attending lectures by Adam Smith. Boswell's father brought him back to school, and after passing his law exam, he returned to London with his father's permission.

In 1763, Boswell met Samuel Johnson, one of the greatest writers of the English language. The two became friends, though Boswell saw Johnson as something of a father figure. In 1764, Boswell began his Grand Tour of Europe, staying a year in Germany and then traveling to Switzerland, Italy, Corsica, and France. On this trip, he met other giants of the Enlightenment, including Jean-Jacques Rousseau and Voltaire. In 1766, he returned home and completed his study in law at the University of Edinburgh, becoming an advocate.

Boswell's contributions to the Enlightenment and Western civilization were not completely apparent while he was alive, but in his last years, he completed his masterwork, *Life of Samuel Johnson*, a biography of his friend. Many consider it to be the greatest biography in the English language. The book was published in 1791 and became an instant critical and commercial success. (Johnson had died in 1784.) The book was unlike any biography before it. Boswell used quotations that he had written down directly from Johnson. Instead of providing a simple fact-based summary of Johnson's life, he provided an intimate portrayal of the writer. Boswell also kept extensive journals throughout his life, and these detailed accounts of his life, thoughts, travels, and interactions with some of the most important people of his time have been a wealth of information for later historians.

Adam Smith

Born in 1723, the son of an advocate, Adam Smith entered the University of Glasgow when he was fourteen. There, Smith came under the spell of Francis Hutcheson and developed his interest in reason, liberties, and the rights of man, with a particular interest in economics. He would, like many of his fellow students, refer to their mentor as "the never to be forgotten Hutcheson."

Smith went on to study at Oxford but found the university stifling. The greatest benefit of his studies there was the use of the extensive Bodleian Library. Under the patronage of Lord Kames, he began delivering lectures at the University of Edinburgh after graduating.

In 1751, Smith took a position teaching logic at Glasgow University. The next year, he was made a member of the Philosophical Society of Edinburgh. In 1759, he published *The Theory of Moral Sentiments*, which provided many of the philosophical foundations of his later works. This book garnered Smith a lot of attention, and he became a favorite teacher in Glasgow.

In 1762, he was offered the job of tutoring Henry Scott, the young Duke of Buccleuch. This allowed him to travel throughout Europe. In Paris, he met the diplomat Benjamin Franklin. After four years, Smith's tutoring assignment ended, and he returned to Scotland to work on his greatest work, *An Inquiry into the Nature and Causes of the Wealth of Nations,* published in 1776.

This book, often shortened to *The Wealth of Nations*, would prove exceptionally influential, especially in the world of economics. It was a paradigm shift, moving away from the *mercantilism* of the past and focusing on a new system to understand the growing commercial societies that Kame had identified as the last stage of civilization.

Smith noted, among many things, the importance of the division of labor to increase production. He explained that the wages for labor depend upon competition among laborers and masters. He explained how workers could combine and no longer compete and that this would drive wages up. When masters combined (which he explained happened much more than people believed), wages decreased. He warned against the influence of special interest groups to stifle a nation's economy. His work, though laborious on occasion, became the gold standard of classic economics and took its place among books that can safely be said to have changed the world.

The book was a commercial success, which surprised many in Smith's circles. Hume declared it was excellent but too hard for the common reader. Edward Gibbon wrote to Adam Ferguson to exclaim about Smith's work. On the other hand, the *Annual Register* gave Smith's book a negative review. In 1791, the radical Thomas Paine wrote in the *Rights of Man* that the reviewer, believed to be the Whig Edmund Burke, simply lacked the talent to understand the book.

In the years after the publication, Smith was consulted by the British Parliament on economic matters, such as the implementation of new taxes. Smith was praised by Prime Minister William Pitt in 1792, though by then Smith had been dead for two years. The *mercantilism* of the past had given way to the free market vision of Smith and other economists. This attitude was adopted by the British government and helped fuel the expansion of the country's economy during the Industrial Revolution. Smith's common-sense approach to economics is said to have been the reason for his great success but also limited his theories. While Smith was among the first economists, many in economics today believe his ideas are outdated.

David Hume

David Hume was born in 1711 in Edinburgh, spending much of his time at Ninewells, his family's small estate in the borderlands. His father died when he was only two, and his mother became entirely focused on rearing her three children. Seeing promise in her youngest son, Katherine Hume sent not just her older son but young David to the University of Edinburgh when he was only ten.

While his family thought he should go into law, Hume decided instead to be a scholar and philosopher. After a rigorous self-imposed routine of reading and reflection for three years, Hume had a breakthrough that first alarmed him and then set him on his course. He moved to France, where he could live cheaply. He settled in a small village in Anjou, which housed a Jesuit school. Having abandoned the religious teachings of his family and the Kirk, he baited the Jesuits with arguments against their faith.

In his twenty-third year, Hume began writing *A Treatise of Human Nature*. He returned to England in 1737 with his manuscript complete and ready for print. To get it printed, he removed some of the more controversial sections that criticized Christianity. The book was not a great success, and Hume felt like he had failed. He applied for the Chair of Ethics and Pneumatic (Mental) Philosophy at Edinburgh in 1745 but was rejected. Six years later, he was rejected for the Chair of Logic in Glasgow. He would never hold an academic post. The next year, Hume became secretary to his cousin, Lt. General James St. Clair, a role that took him to Austria and Italy.

Humes had more success with later publications, including *An Enquiry Concerning Human Understanding*, *An Enquiry Concerning the Principles of Morals*, and a collection of essays titled *Political Discourses*. Many of these were reworkings of parts he'd taken out of *Treatise*.

He then became the Librarian to the Edinburgh Faculty of Advocates, like Lord Kame before him. Using the library's resources he compiled a book in six volumes. *The History of England* appeared in installments from 1754 to 1762. This became a bestseller and gave him financial independence. Still, he was a known atheist and skeptic and faced charges of excommunication from the Kirk and dismissal from his position.

In 1763, Hume accepted a job as the secretary to the ambassador to France. He became a hit in Parisian salons for his wit, love of good food, and delight in the affections of women. He returned to Scotland and moved into a comfortable house in New Town in Edinburgh. He spent his remaining years editing his works and enjoying the company of friends and acquaintances. In 1775, he was diagnosed with intestinal cancer and arranged for the posthumous publication of a controversial work called *Dialogues Concerning Natural Religion*.

Hume's influence in the realm of philosophy can hardly be understated. Many regard him as one of the greatest philosophers in the English language and one of the most influential in Europe. Many approaches and ideas in philosophy carry the title "Humean," as being influenced or directly pulled from Hume's works. Humes' thoughts on religion and use of rationalism influenced German theology during the German Enlightenment. Hume's *Treatise* has been called the founding document on cognitive science. Immanuel Kant credited Hume with awakening him from his "dogmatic slumber," and Albert Einstein credited Hume's works in helping him create his theory of special relativity. However, Hume's writings on race led to the David Hume Tower of Edinburgh University being renamed by a student-led campaign. Hume was a great philosopher and writer, but like so many historical figures, his views in certain areas failed to age gracefully.

Chapter 9: The Industrial Revolution and Its Impact on Scottish Society

When America won its independence from Britain, the former colony took control of its tobacco trade. Thus, Scotland's near monopoly disappeared overnight. In its place, Scottish merchants focused on the cotton industry. Raw cotton was purchased from the American South and processed in Scotland.

One of the earliest forms of industrialization was the power loom, an automated loom invented by Englishman Edmund Cartwright, which could weave cotton into textiles at an astonishing rate. This allowed the Scottish merchants to sell huge quantities of cotton in a short amount of time.

Cartwright's first mill was built in 1788 and was run by steam power. This revolutionary invention was perfected by James Watt, born in Greenock, Scotland, in 1736. The steam water pump had been invented in the seventeenth century, and the first successful engine was developed by Thomas Newcomen in 1712, but Watt's invention greatly improved the engine to allow it to be utilized in a myriad of different ways. His work on the steam engine turned it from a small novelty to the force behind the industrial revolution.

The Boulton-Watt engine, named after Watt and Matthew Boulton, who supported the inventor's years of trial and error, was first used as a pump for mines in 1776. Watt improved his invention again, and in 1782, a Boulton-Watt engine was used at a sawmill, where it replaced twelve horses. Watt also created the concept of "horsepower," meaning the sawmill engine had twelve horsepower. By 1800, eight-four British cotton mills used Boulton-Watt engines. Soon, steam engines based on Watt's design were used to turn paddles, creating steamboats. Then steam engines were used to produce locomotives and begin the railroad industry.

James Watt, Scottish inventor.

Watt was an undeniable genius. While still quite young, he attracted the attention of Glasgow professors Joseph Black, the famed chemist, and the equally well-known Adam Smith, who both became Watt's friends and supporters. Watt also invented the pounds per square inch (psi), which is still used today to measure pressure. The "watt," a unit of power, is named after the inventor. He was one of the first people to create and use bleach to whiten textiles. Watt was a member of the Lunar Society of Birmingham, which was a dinner club of industrialists and other important figures at the beginning of the Industrial Revolution. He retired in 1800, a relatively wealthy man.

The cotton industry in Scotland would eventually be eclipsed by iron, steel, coal, engineering, and shipbuilding. The area along the River Clyde soon became a world leader in shipbuilding. Bridges and canals were built to ease the movement of goods and people.

While Scotland became more industrialized, Scottish farmers also looked to new methods for raising crops and livestock. In the Highlands, the previous attempts to undermine the clan system had been largely successful. Clan chiefs turned into landlords who found the best use of their land was keeping herds of sheep. They evicted many of their residents. Whole villages were depopulated, and the ousted Highlanders had little choice but to immigrate to America or join the growing populations of Scottish cities. Within the cities, numbers were drastically rising. Glasgow, home to only 12,000 people in 1707, had a population of 77,000 by 1810 and 300,000 by 1830. In 1760, Edinburgh had a population of 50,000. Forty years later, that number had doubled.

It was not just Highlanders flocking to cities but also Irish immigrants looking for more opportunities and later fleeing the potato famine of the 1840s. These industrialized urban centers became overcrowded and led to appalling living conditions that directly affected the health of the population. Disease ran rampant. Mortality rates soared. The influx of laborers, as Adam Smith would have predicted, caused a drop in wages.

By the end of the eighteenth century, driven by the threat of power looms and steam engines that put them out of their jobs, Scottish cotton weavers formed one of the first trade unions. However, it wasn't until later in the nineteenth century that the trade union movement really took off. The Scottish Miners' Federation was founded in 1886. Around the same time, the Scottish Labor Party was formed, with one of its stated aims being home rule for Scotland. It did not last long and was absorbed into the larger British Labor Party.

The ideals of the Enlightenment were not abandoned during the Industrial Revolution. One of the greatest proponents of Francis Hutcheson and Adam Smith in the early nineteenth century was the University of Edinburgh Professor Dugald Stewart. Stewart was a popular and influential teacher, but he is perhaps best known for who he taught. Some of his pupils were Francis Horner, Francis Jeffery, Henry Thomas Cockburn, Henry Brougham, and the Englishman Sydney Smith. Several of these individuals would have stunning political careers as prime ministers and lord chancellors. In fact, for part of the nineteenth century, the British Parliament was dominated by Scotsmen.

Yet, what this group did before embarking on their political careers is what they might be best known for: the creation of the *Edinburgh Review*, or more accurately, the third version of the *Edinburgh Review*. This magazine, which ran from 1802 to 1929, was a great promoter of Whig or liberal politics and Romanticism. It could be highly critical, especially to the Lake Poets, including William Wordsworth. The *Review* was an instant success and helped launch the careers of many great writers, including William Makepeace Thackeray, William Hazlitt, John Stuart Mill, and the greatest writer of the age (and a former student of Dugald Stewart), Sir Walter Scott.

Born in 1771 in Edinburgh's Old Town, Walter Scott was the ninth son of an advocate. He contracted polio when he was young, which gave him a life-long limp. Shortly thereafter, he was sent to live with his grandparents thirty miles outside of Edinburgh. There, he regained his health and became enamored with reading and hearing Scottish legends from his aunt Jenny and grandmother Barbara. He began writing poetry.

Scott returned to Edinburgh in 1778, where his family was now living in a larger house in New Town. He attended the high school and received tutoring in writing and arithmetic. He went to live with his Aunt Jenny again for a few months in Kelso and there met a good friend and future business partner, James Ballantyne. He attended the University of Edinburgh and eventually decided to study law. He then met the great Scottish poet, Robert Burns.

Scott completed his studies in 1792 and began working as a lawyer while translating German poems into English in his spare time. In 1809, he joined Ballantyne as a silent partner in a publishing house, John Ballantyne & Co. Through this publishing house, Scott began to publish poems, notably *Lady of the Lake*. In 1808, he published *Marmion* about the battle between the English and Scots at Flodden Field in 1513. This contained one of his most often quoted phrases, "Oh! What a tangled web we weave/ when first we practice to deceive!"

In 1814, his first novel, *Waverley*, was published anonymously. The book was a great success, and he followed it up with more in the series, though each was published under a pseudonym. Most people began to suspect that Scott was the author, but he did not publicly acknowledge the fact until 1827.

In 1818, the prince regent (later George IV) was so impressed with Scott's talents that he allowed the writer to search Edinburgh Castle for the lost royal Scottish regalia, last seen after the passing of the Act of Union of 1707. Scott eventually found the regalia in an oak chest, wrapped in linen just as they had been over a hundred years before. Scott was awarded a baronet and was heavily involved in planning George IV's visit to Scotland in 1820, the first visit from a Hanoverian monarch.

Scott continued writing, producing international bestsellers like *Ivanhoe*, *Rob Roy*, and *The Heart of Midlothian*. He became one of the most popular writers of his time and is often credited with inventing historical fiction. He became an exemplar of European Romanticism and became a force for preserving a mythical version of Scottish history that seemed to criticize the industrialization and urbanization of the country during the nineteenth century. At the very least, Scott offered his readers a romantic version of Scottish history.

It was during the period just before and after Scott's works that the "Clearances" of the Highlands took place. As previously mentioned, clan chieftains took on the role of landlords and found it was more lucrative to keep sheep than people, evicting large numbers of people from their ancestral lands. They were sent to coastal villages, where they were expected to fish, gather kelp to sell, or farm much smaller plots of land called crofts. It soon became apparent that there was not enough work in these crofting villages, and many people had no choice but to emigrate either to Scottish cities or, more often, North America—especially Nova Scotia. The Highland society that Scott had popularized in his works was quickly disappearing, if it had even really existed at all. Later, the Highland Potato Famine finalized the Clearances.

Still, the country, especially the Lowlands, provided fertile ground for the Industrial Revolution. There was abundant and cheap labor available. Scottish banks were more lightly regulated than their English counterparts, and this allowed for tremendous financial growth.

Scotland enjoyed a large coastline, and almost every area of the country was easily reachable via ships, canals, roads, and eventually railroads. Scotland employed the use of turnpikes, where private companies could build roads and charge reasonable tolls for their use. This resulted in a wide network of maintained roads that could be used for transport.

Scottish merchants traded in a wide variety of commodities, including leather, sugar, rope, and linen goods. They bought sugar from plantations in the West Indies and sold it to dealers in Britain for high prices thanks to the skyrocketing demand. Factories in Scotland included glassworks, iron foundries, and sailmakers. There were breweries, whisky distilleries, and soap makers as well.

Coal mining became a major industry. Scotland went from producing one million tons of coal out of five different coal fields in 1775 to over three million in 1830. Production would peak at 142 million tons per year in the twentieth century. By 1860, Scotland contained 171 iron furnaces and produced over a million tons of pig iron a year.

The first railroad in Scotland was between Monkland and Kirkintilloch, built in 1826. In the 1840s, railway building increased dramatically, putting Scotland in competition with its southern neighbor for the number of lines and services. The North British Railway connected eastern Scotland with Newcastle, and the Caledonian Railway connected Glasgow and Carlisle. By the 1860s, a series of mergers meant that five companies owned 98 percent of the rail lines in Scotland.

In 1850, 32 percent of Scotland's population lived in a city. By 1900, 50 percent of the population was urban. Glasgow had become the largest city with a population approaching one million by 1900. It was one of the largest cities in the world and was considered the "Second City of the Empire" after London. Dundee, on the east coast of Scotland, emerged as an urban center thanks to an expanded harbor and the growth of the three main industries of the city: jute, jam, and journalism. The jam specifically refers to marmalade, which was first commercially made in Dundee in the eighteenth century.

Yet, in Dundee, Glasgow, Aberdeen, and other growing cities, living conditions continued to decline. Infant mortality was much higher in Scottish cities during the Industrial Revolution than in English or other European cities. Overall mortality was also exceptionally high. The death rate was at its highest in the 1840s due to an influx of Irish immigrants and Highlanders escaping the potato famines. This was finally curbed thanks to advancements in medicine.

In fact, Scotland had a long history of medical developments, beginning with John and William Hunter, brothers from Calderwood in East Kilbride. Surgeons, physicians, and anatomists, the brothers helped advance medicine in Britain—largely due to the availability of human cadavers for dissection. The use of cadavers was not frowned upon in Scotland as it was in England. This eventually led to great discoveries but also the infamous case of Burke and Hare, who murdered victims to provide bodies to Dr. Knox in Edinburgh in the 1820s.

One of the more famous Scottish physicians of the nineteenth century was Sir Charles Bell. Born in Edinburgh in 1774, Charles came from a distinguished family of surgeons and lawyers. He was also another student of Dugald Stewart. Charles was forced to leave Edinburgh and go to London due to a feud one of his older brothers had with faculty members of the University of Edinburgh. Bell joined the Hunterian School of Medicine founded by William Hunter. He was present at the Battle of Waterloo, where he acted as a battlefield surgeon. He used his artistic abilities to give new insight into the inner workings of the body as well as many illnesses and how they affected his patients.

Charles Bell is not to be confused with Benjamin Bell, an associate of John Hunter and Scottish physician William Cullen. Benjamin, born in Dumfries in 1749, was the first scientific Scottish surgeon and founded a dynasty of doctors, including his great-grandson, Joseph Bell. Joseph was renowned for his diagnostic abilities and regularly astonished his pupils, including a young Arthur Conan Doyle, who used Dr. Bell as the basis for the character of Sherlock Holmes.

Perhaps one of the most interesting narratives of Scotland in the Industrial Revolution began with a man named George Lauder, who was born in Dunfermline in 1815. George's father owned a snuff mill, and when George became an adult, he started a general store on High Street in his hometown. George was a Chartist, which meant he believed in universal suffrage for all male citizens of the United Kingdom. This was a working-class movement named after the People's Charter of 1838. At the time, only landowners could vote. This excluded a huge swath of the population, especially disenfranchised urban voters.

George was also a champion of education rights for all Scots and was closely aligned with radical liberals like his father-in-law, the firebrand Thomas Morrison. He was also a Scottish nationalist. George had only one child, a son named George Lauder Jr. He also helped to support and educate his two nephews, Andrew and Thomas. His son was very close to his cousin Andrew, and the two grew like brothers. However, when Andrew was twelve, his family had to borrow money from George Lauder Sr. and immigrate to Allegheny, Pennsylvania.

In America, Andrew began to work to help support his family, first at a Scottish-owned cotton mill and then as a messenger boy in a telegraph office. This young Scottish-born boy, whose full name was Andrew Carnegie, was beginning a journey that would lead him to become one of the world's wealthiest men. He would later make his cousin, George Lauder Jr., a partner in his businesses.

However, Carnegie did not forget the lessons learned in his uncle's general store. Knowing the difference that a helping hand could make, he spent much of his fortune on philanthropic works. He drew inspiration from the tales of William Wallace, Robert Bruce, and Rob Roy. He understood the importance of education and built libraries in countless towns across America. However, what his uncle might have thought of his exploitation of workers is unknown.

Chapter 10: Modern Scotland — Devolution, National Identity, and the Quest for Independence

Since the Act of Union in 1707, many Scots have dreamed of an independent Scotland.

The urbanization, growth, and industrialization of Scotland led to a government crisis in the management of Scottish affairs by the authorities of Great Britain. Certain agencies were created to deal with the pressing needs of the Scottish population, including the Board of Supervision for Poor Relief (created in 1845), the General Board of Commissioners in Lunacy (1857), and the Scottish Education Department as part of the Privy Council (1872).

However, these agencies had little oversight and accountability. Scottish MPs requested that the British government create a Secretary of Scotland, which was finally created in 1885 as the Scottish Office, run by the Secretary of State of Scotland. Under this new office, various government bodies were consolidated and reformed to better serve the Scottish population, which continued to increase. (The year 1901 brought the highest increase of 10 percent.) By the early twentieth century, boards of health, agriculture, and prisons were created by the Reorganization of Offices Act of 1928.

Still, the advocates of home rule were not satisfied. In 1907, another small step was taken in the creation of the Scottish Committee in the

House of Commons. Scottish members could deal with Scottish bills that might be presented to the whole legislative body.

With the outbreak of war in 1914, Scotland's problems seemed less pressing, and Scots answered the call to support the United Kingdom on every front of the war effort. There were thirty-five Scottish battalions in World War I. They served on the Western Front, in Egypt, in Palestine, and in defending Britain. There were the Highlanders and The Royal Scots, among others.

The toll that the war took on the Scottish people was severe. In some cases, all the male members of a single family were wiped out throughout the war. The exact number of Scots who died in World War I is not yet known, but it is believed to be over one hundred thousand. It was not just the war that claimed Scots but the outbreak of an influenza pandemic misleadingly called the "Spanish flu." Scotland had a period of high death rates and decreased birth and marriage rates as a result. Still, Scotland's population reached a record of 4.8 million in 1919. At the same time, the end of the war led to a "baby boom," and 1920 holds the record for the most births in a single year at 137,000.

The interwar period for Scotland did not bring the boom and bust of the United States or Germany but the perhaps more tragic dismantling of the economy. Generally, economic growth was slow in the United Kingdom after the First World War, but it was especially sluggish in Scotland. Wages and salaries barely increased in the 1920s. After the onset of the global Great Depression in 1929, Scottish incomes fell drastically. Unemployment skyrocketed in Scotland and quickly outpaced the rest of the United Kingdom. Scotland was also slower to recover. In 1934, for instance, Great Britain had an estimated unemployment rate of 16.6 percent, which is certainly high. In the same year, Scotland had an unemployment rate of 23.2 percent, and its rate did not return to the 1929 figures until 1936, four years after the rest of the country.

It has been speculated that the reason for this downturn was Scotland's reliance on heavy industry and a lack of diversification among its industries. However, research has shown that Scotland's industries were just as diversified as England's, the main difference being Scotland's much slower growth. The reality was more complicated. Scotland had a large number of jobs in declining or depressed industries that were particularly susceptible to economic distress. One example is shipbuilding, which was much more important in Scotland than in England or Wales. When the demand for ships rapidly decreased after World War I, Scotland was hit especially hard. Since many other industries in Scotland also relied on business from shipbuilders and their employees, they suffered as well.

Scotland's population growth also suffered at this time. In fact, from 1921 to 1931, the population decreased by 0.9 percent. This was the first recorded drop in the country's population since the first census records of the early nineteenth century.

Many Scots blamed London for their woes, and the idea of home rule was revived. London responded with another small step by making the Scottish Secretary a Cabinet rank with wider powers. Scotland thus gained more administrative independence, but the new Nationalists wanted nothing less than complete political independence.

In 1934, the Scottish National Party was formed from the merger of two nationalist groups. The party had been conceived by John MacCormick, a lawyer from the University of Glasgow who wanted to raise the question of home rule above party loyalties in Scotland. The movement had strong support and strong leadership. The first presidents of the party were James Graham, 6th Duke of Montrose, and Robert Cunninghame Graham. Montrose was a naval officer and politician who was the first to take a photo of a solar eclipse and is credited with the invention of the aircraft carrier. Graham, who was not related to the duke, was an adventurer and socialist politician. Both men were keenly devoted to Scottish home rule. However, events on the continent in 1939 would once again undermine the home rule cause.

The Nationalists did not want Scotland to be a completely independent state. "Home rule" was a phrase used to indicate a political situation in which Scotland would have autonomy to govern itself while remaining part of the United Kingdom and receiving the protections the UK offered. This meant that when World War II broke out in 1939, most Scottish men expected to fight for Great Britain against her enemies. One of the Scottish National Party leaders, Douglas Young, argued that Scottish people should refuse conscription into the armed forces. But he was vilified for undermining the war effort and thus helping the Axis powers. Young was imprisoned for his beliefs.

John MacCormick left the party in 1942 because he could not steer the SNP to home rule, which was believed to be supported by most Scottish people. The SNP instead adopted the more radical position of complete independence from the UK. MacCormick argued for a "devolved"

Scottish Assembly and formed the Scottish Covenant Association. (Devolution is the statutory delegation of powers from a central government to a more local level. It is often compared to the concept of home rule in Scotland.)The name of the Scottish Covenant Association was chosen to directly reference the Covenanters of the sixteenth and seventeenth centuries.

Like their forefathers, the association created a new Scottish Covenant to be signed by the public, this time in support of devolution. Written in 1949 at the Church of Scotland Assembly Halls in Edinburgh, the document was eventually signed by over two million people—a little less than half the population of Scotland. However, the petition had little political impact.

In the 1960s, support for Home Rule gained support in political circles. Finally, in 1978, the Scotland Act was passed, which would establish a devolved legislative body in Scotland as long as it was approved by 40 percent of the Scottish electorate. A consequent referendum, however, failed to produce the needed votes. The proposed Scottish Assembly was not created, and the act was repealed.

This might have been the end of the idea of home rule, but there was still a strong current within Scottish society that longed for the authority to at least partially govern themselves. This finally came with the Scotland Act of 1998, which was supported by a referendum held in 1997 showing that most Scots were in favor of home rule. This act created a new Scottish Parliament within Scotland with legislative and taxing powers. It was the most significant piece of legislation for Scotland since the Act of Union in 1707.

The Scottish Parliament meets in the Holyrood area of Edinburgh and is often called "Holyrood" for that reason. There are 129 democratically elected members of the parliament. The Scottish National Party, as of 2021, holds the plurality of seats.

In line with this new independence, the Stone of Scone was finally returned to Scotland in 1996 in acknowledgment of Scottish heritage and the cultural significance of the object. Interestingly, the stone had been stolen from England by Scottish Nationalists in 1950 but returned four months later—though some suggest the stone returned was not the original stone. The stone was brought out in 2023 for the crowning of King Charles III.

Another possible reason for the change of public opinion on home rule from the early 1970s to the 1990s was the discovery of oil in the North Sea off the coast of Scotland in the mid-1970s. The Scottish National Party pushed hard with the slogan "It's Scotland's oil," attempting to convince the public that the Scottish people would not enjoy the benefits of the oil without a devolved legislative body. It is also worth noting that, over time, the SNP stepped back from its position on complete independence. This also helped lead to the creation of the Scottish Parliament.

While Scottish population growth has not boomed in the twenty-first century, the population enjoys a steady growth rate. The heavy industries of the Industrial Revolution have not made a comeback in the country, but new industries have begun. Silicon Glen is a high-tech sector of businesses from Dundee to Edinburgh and Inverclyde, including Stirling, Glasgow, and Fife.

The development of Silicon Glen hails back to post-World War II when Ferranti moved an electronic plant to Edinburgh. Silicon Glen produced semiconductors, largely in Glenrothes. The sector was hit hard by the technology collapse of 2000, but Scotland had learned from previous eras. Thanks to the diversification of industries, the country was not largely affected. Since then, Silicon Glen has bounced back, with plants being built by foreign companies like Amazon and the development of local businesses.

While Scotland's future is unknown, there remains reason to be hopeful.

Conclusion

While it is a small nation, roughly equivalent in size to the US state of South Carolina, Scotland has had a great impact on Europe and the rest of the world. Over the years, many Scots have emigrated to places like the United States, Canada, Australia, and New Zealand. There are many more people of Scottish descent living abroad than the five million that call Scotland home.

In the same way, Scotland's ideas and inventions have spread around the world. The Church of Scotland is in every Presbyterian church. The principles of liberty and self-governance that Scottish thinkers first expressed have become the cornerstones of other nations' constitutions. Scots have contributed the pedal bicycle and the pneumatic tire, the condensing steam engine of James Watt, the first iron-hulled ship, wire rope, the telephone (Alexander Graham Bell was born in Scotland), the BBC, radar, postcards, modern economics, modern geology, the hypodermic syringe, and fried chicken. In the world of domestic appliances, the Scots seemed particularly adept at inventing not just the refrigerator but also the flush toilet, the lawnmower, and the television.

While Scotland struggled after 1707 to regain its independence from England, one could easily argue that in the intervening years, Scottish politicians, businessmen, and writers slowly conquered their southern neighbor without the need for an army.

There is reason to believe, with the current state of affairs, that the Scottish people will be content with their situation. However, a study of Scottish history tells any student who is paying attention that the Scots are never idle for long. They will, one way or another, make themselves known. Scots tend to come onto the scene, whether through art or science, industry or politics, and solve a problem that has been troubling people for generations or, perhaps, introduce a problem that no one was even aware of. This is one of the lasting benefits of Scotland and the Scottish people. Their rich heritage and their desire for liberty—however they might define it—drives them to prove themselves repeatedly, and the world is often, but not always, the better for it.

While it is easy to get lost in the triumphs of Scotland, like the fight for independence from England, or its romantic failures, like the tale of Bonnie Prince Charlie, we must not forget that Scotland carries the stains of the era of colonization. Scottish merchants traded in human beings, and many Scottish immigrants to British colonies waged merciless war on indigenous people. However, Scotland shows every indication of carrying this shame honorably. In keeping with the strange nature of the country, Scots can also empathize with those they helped to conquer because they themselves were conquered many times. Scotland's history is that of a country oppressed but regularly breaking through that oppression by force, will, or wit alone.

Think of the Highlanders—not the Hollywood version, but the real thing. They lived a mean existence, but they could trace their line back to noble blood. It is hard not to like a group of self-reliant people who spend their time fighting each other over every slight but, when an outside force threatens their homes, come together to send the invaders running. Even in defeat, they can fade into the mountains and glens, only to regroup and continue the fight.

The Lowlander, not often celebrated in verse or on the big screen, is just as appealing. Often, they were hard workers with an appreciation for equal education, through which the lowest laborer could often quote Latin or at least read and write. From their numbers came some of the greatest thinkers of the Enlightenment who truly reshaped the world with words and ideas. Poets, novelists, dukes, tinkerers, and merchants who could buy and sell them all, all called Scotland home.

From the clear waters of mountain rivers to the dirty streets of Victorian Edinburgh, Scotland has managed to enchant many people the world over. Her history tells a story of struggle, failure, and triumph that resonates with any breathing person. This book is just a small portion of the great history of the country. We hope it encourages you to investigate the history of Scotland even further.

Part 2: Scottish Mythology

Enthralling Myths, Folktales, and Legends from Scotland

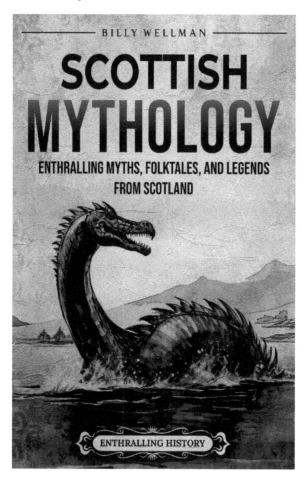

Introduction

Scottish mythology is deeply rooted in Celtic mythology, sharing common threads with its Irish counterpart while also possessing unique elements. Historically speaking, the Celts originated in central Europe during the Late Bronze Age, around 1200 BCE. They were not a unified nation but rather a collection of tribes sharing linguistic, cultural, and social similarities. Their society was characterized by a rich oral tradition, skilled craftsmanship, and a complex religious system with druids as spiritual leaders.

Over time, the Celts began to expand their territory. However, their migration was not a single, coordinated movement; instead, it was a series of waves that spanned several centuries. These migrations were driven by various factors, including the need for more space due to booming populations, the allure of trade, and perhaps the search for lands suitable for farming. By the Iron Age, around 800 BCE, Celtic tribes had spread across a large part of western Europe, even reaching Britain and Ireland.

The Celts' arrival in Scotland is pieced together from archaeological findings and historical deductions, as there are no written records from the Celts themselves during that time. It is believed they arrived in Scotland sometime during the last few centuries before the Common Era began. What we can be sure of, however, is that their arrival marked significant cultural shifts, with the local people of Scotland starting to adopt Celtic languages, artistic styles, and social systems.

As the Celts settled in Scotland, their myths and legends became deeply rooted in the Scottish landscape. The gods, heroes, and mythical creatures of Celtic lore were adapted to the Scottish environment, embodying the features of its mountains, forests, and lochs. The natural world was central to Celtic spirituality, and this connection is vividly reflected in Scottish mythology.

The spread of Celtic influence in Scotland was not just cultural but also linguistic. The Celtic languages, part of the Indo-European language family, diversified into several branches, with Gaelic becoming dominant in Scotland. This language carried with it the stories, poems, and songs that formed the backbone of Celtic mythology.

It's important to note that the Celtic influence in Scotland was not a case of cultural replacement but one of integration and synthesis. The existing beliefs and traditions of Scotland's indigenous populations melded with those of the Celts, creating a unique cultural and mythological identity.

In Scottish mythology, you find unique entities like the Kelpie, a shape-shifting water spirit, and the Cailleach, an ancient hag representing the harshness of winter. These figures, while uniquely Scottish, echo the broader Celtic fascination with nature and its spirits.

The similarities with Irish myths are also seen in shared characters and motifs. For instance, the Irish hero Fionn mac Cumhaill appears in Scottish tales too, albeit with variations. Likewise, the concept of the Otherworld, a mystical realm inhabited by deities and the dead, is prominent in both mythologies.

Both Scottish and Irish myths emphasize the power of storytelling and oral tradition. These stories were passed down through the generations and were more than just entertainment; they were a way of understanding the world and conveying social and moral lessons.

For example, the tragic love tale of Deirdre and Naoise is one of the most popular tales that has been passed down through the ages. It has themes of love, freedom, and destiny, all of which resonate deeply in both Scottish and Irish folklore, illustrating the often-tragic nature of love and the cruel twists of fate. In contrast, the tale of Thomas Rhymer and the Queen of Elfland offers a different perspective. Thomas Rhymer, a bard known for his prophetic talents, encounters the Queen of Elfland, a mystical figure from the Otherworld. She invites him to her realm, where he stays for seven years. Unlike Deirdre and Naoise's story, this tale is not marked by tragedy but rather by enchantment and mystery.

Witchcraft, dark magic, and ghostly apparitions also hold a prominent place in the rich fabric of old Scottish beliefs. In Scottish folklore, witchcraft was often viewed with a mixture of fear and awe, with witches depicted as possessing powerful abilities. The late 16th and early 17th centuries witnessed intense witch hunts, reflecting societal fears and religious influences.

Ghosts in Scottish lore, on the other hand, are frequently tied to specific locations like castles and ancient sites. Tales of restless spirits often serve as moral lessons about the consequences of one's actions. Similarly, curses in Scottish myths are seen as powerful forces capable of bringing misfortune, underscoring the belief in the power of words and spells.

In short, the origin of the Celts in central Europe and their gradual migration to Scotland brought about a rich cultural heritage. The migration of the Celts to Scotland is a story of cultural blending, where old tales were reshaped and evolved, resonating across the highlands and lochs and shaping the very soul of Scottish mythology.

Chapter 1: The Beginning: Creation Myths and the Scottish Landscape

In the far north of Europe, where ancient mountains rise like silent guardians and lochs lie deep and mysterious, lies Scotland. Its rugged beauty, carved over millennia, tells a story older than time. To understand its formation, we must first embark on a journey back to the Ice Age. It was a time when great sheets of ice as thick as mountains covered the land. These glaciers moved slowly but sculpted the valleys and hills, leaving behind a landscape both harsh and breathtaking.

However, there is another tale, one woven into the very fabric of Scottish folklore, about the shaping of this land. It speaks of the Cailleach, also known as Beira, the ancient hag and the creator and shaper of mountains and valleys. Her story is one of magic and mystery, an intricate blend of the harsh realities of nature and the rich imagination of the ancient peoples.

The Cailleach was no ordinary figure. She was the embodiment of winter and the land's wild, untamed nature. Her appearance was as formidable as the elements she controlled. She was often depicted as a giantess, towering over the landscape, her skin as pale as snow and as rough as the rugged mountainsides. Her eyes, piercing and blue, mirrored the icy lochs and the winter sky. Her hair, long and white, flowed like the cascading waterfalls, and her voice was like the howling wind.

A 1917 illustration of the Cailleach.

With a hammer made of thunder and lightning, the Cailleach roamed the land, sculpting its features. One legend explains how Scotland turned into the rugged landscape that we see today. The Cailleach roamed the lands of Scotland with a large creel, or wicker basket, filled with rocks and stones. These weren't ordinary rocks; they were the building blocks of the land itself, charged with the magic and might of this ancient deity. As she traversed the rugged terrain, her task was to create and shape the features of the land, such as its mountains, hills, and valleys.

However, as she journeyed across Scotland, occasionally, either through carelessness or due to the sheer weight of her burden, rocks fell from her basket. Each rock, which was imbued with her power, transformed into a part of the landscape. Where a large stone fell, a mountain would rise, rugged and majestic. Smaller stones formed hills, and the smallest pebbles became boulders and crags.

This process, repeated over time, led to the formation of Scotland's unique and varied topography. This story elegantly blends the idea of an accidental yet fateful creation with the deliberate shaping of the land. It paints the Cailleach not only as a creator but also as an elemental force whose actions, whether intentional or not, have profound impacts on the natural world.

The Cailleach was also the powerful being that was responsible for the creation of Scotland's very first loch. According to folktales, there was a magical well on top of Ben Cruachan, a mountain. Each night, the divine hag had to cap the well to prevent it from overflowing, and each morning, she removed the cap so that the water could flow. However, on one fateful night, the Cailleach accidentally skipped her routine. Perhaps exhausted by her daily labors, the hag fell into a deep sleep, forgetting to cover the well.

The water from the well began to flow unchecked the entire night. It gushed forth in torrents, cascading down the mountainside with unstoppable force. By the time the Cailleach rose from her slumber, the water had formed an immense loch in the valley below. This great body of water became known as Loch Awe.

The revered hag goddess of winter also played a pivotal role in the changing of the seasons. As autumn's colors faded and winter's chill began to whisper across the valleys, the Cailleach was said to move to the Gulf of Corryvreckan. Here, amidst the roaring waters, she washed her immense great plaid, a significant task that ushered in the transformation of autumn's twilight into winter's deep embrace.

Legend has it that Corryvreckan, with its fierce and swirling currents, became her washtub. The whirlpool, known for its thunderous roar, is a permanent feature of the landscape. Although the whirlpool is always present, its visibility and intensity vary with the tides. Some claim the sound could reach distances as far as twenty miles away and lasted for three full days.

The Corryvreckan whirlpool, believed to be the Cailleach's washtub.
Walter Baxter / The Corryvreckan Whirlpool:
https://commons.wikimedia.org/wiki/File:The_Corryvreckan_Whirlpool_-_geograph-2404815-by-Walter-Baxter.jpg

Once done, the great plaid would be pure white, as it had been thoroughly cleansed in the churning waters. This cloth, transformed by the old goddess's hands, then became the expansive blanket of snow that gently covered the land.

The Cailleach was more than just a creator; she was a guardian of animals and a protector of the wild. She nurtured the deer and the wild goats, and her presence was felt in the rustling of leaves and the whispering of the wind. Her persona was complex. She could be fierce and formidable, like the storms of winter, but she could also be nurturing and protective, like a mother to the land and its creatures.

Legends say that the Cailleach would transform into a beautiful young woman once every hundred years, but she would age rapidly as the seasons turned. This cycle symbolized the eternal rhythm of nature, the never-ending dance of creation and destruction, life and death, and winter and spring.

A Battle between Two Giants: Benandonner and Finn McCool

Benandonner, known as the Red Man of Antrim, was a being of immense size and power. His home was among the towering cliffs and deep valleys of Scotland, a land as hard and unyielding as the giant himself. Legends of his strength and valor were as common as the heather on the hillsides.

Across the narrow sea lay Ireland, home to another giant, Finn McCool. Although Benandonner had never met Finn, he had heard tales of his Irish counterpart. Finn McCool, also known in Gaelic as Fionn mac Cumhaill, was not just any giant. He was a warrior, a leader, and a man of great wisdom and bravery. His feats were the stuff of legend, and his valor was celebrated in the Celts' fireside tales.

The tale we are recounting began in Ireland, where Finn, standing on the rugged cliffs, would often gaze across the North Channel toward Scotland, wondering about the giant he had heard of but never seen. Finn, whose pride was as great as his stature, grew restless with the thought of another giant who might match or even surpass his strength. Although Finn was said to have lived peacefully with his wife Oonagh, Benandonner's continuous taunts shouted from across the sea eventually led to Finn's fury.

Every day, the two giants exchanged insults, both shouting at the top of their lungs. Eventually, they began to hurl rocks at each other. However, their throws were not powerful enough; the distance between them was too vast. Finn once threw a lump of land toward Scotland, but it fell short. Landing in the middle of the ocean, this great lump of land formed the Isle of Man. The location from where the lump of land was collected was filled with water, becoming what we know today as Lough Neagh.

There was no sign that the rivalry between the two would cool down. Perhaps driven by a desire to prove himself the greatest giant in the land and to teach the mysterious Scottish giant a lesson for taunting him, Finn finally decided to challenge Benandonner to a face-to-face battle. But there was one problem that stopped him from doing so: the vicious sea that lay between them. However, Finn was never known to back down. Days later, the undeterred giant eventually came up with an idea. He collected his strength and began to pick up huge chunks of the Irish coast and throw them into the roaring sea. These stones formed a causeway that stretched all the way to Scotland.

Meanwhile, in Scotland, Benandonner saw this path forming and understood Finn's challenge. Burning with his own pride and the fire of competition, Benandonner started his journey across the causeway toward Ireland, eager to meet Finn in battle. This was the exact moment when

Finn finally understood the humongous size of Benandonner; the Scottish giant was way larger than him. Benandonner's stomp on the causeway could shake the very ocean that separated their lands. For the first time in his life, Finn felt a touch of fear.

Finn rushed to his dwelling, where his dearest wife, Oonagh, was waiting for him. In an almost trembling voice, Finn told his wife about Benandonner and his fearsome size. The Irish giant was terrified of his fate, as he was confident that it would be nearly impossible to defeat Benandonner in battle. Thankfully, Oonagh was renowned for her beauty and her cunning mind. Upon listening to her husband's worry, the giantess quickly devised a plan and chose to use cunning to outwit brute strength. First, Oonagh dressed Finn as a baby, swaddling him in an enormous blanket and placing him in a massive cradle. The disguise had to be convincing; Benandonner was no fool.

When Benandonner arrived in front of their door, Oonagh welcomed him with warmth. She explained that Finn was out on an errand but would return shortly. As they waited, she gestured toward the cradle, introducing the disguised Finn as their baby. Benandonner was surprised when he saw the huge infant.

"If this was the size of their baby, how big could the father be?" Benandonner thought to himself. The sight of the "baby" was definitely intended to sow a seed of doubt in Benandonner's mind about the size and strength of his rival. However, this was not enough to send the Scottish giant back to where he came from.

So, Oonagh went on with her plan. She offered him an oatmeal cake, a common treat in those parts. But this was no ordinary cake. Oonagh had cunningly baked a large iron griddle into the center of the cake. When the unsuspecting Benandonner bit into it, he let out a roar of pain as his tooth shattered against the hidden metal.

She had also presented a soft, griddle-free cake to the "baby" Finn. The disguised giant easily bit into it, exacerbating the illusion of the child's strength. Benandonner watched in astonishment and growing trepidation as the "infant" munched happily on the cake, a task Benandonner had found painfully impossible. Again, his mind raced with thoughts of how formidable Finn must be if his child possessed such strength.

But Oonagh wasn't finished yet. She handed a "rock," which was, in fact, a lump of soft cheese, to the disguised Finn, casually mentioning how Finn had taught their son to squeeze juice from a stone. Finn squeezed the cheese, making it appear as if he was extracting liquid from a rock.

Benandonner was intrigued. He attempted to replicate the feat with a real rock. He let out deep grunts as he strained and struggled, yet no juice came forth. The implications were clear to the Scottish giant. If a mere infant could perform such a feat, what kind of monstrous strength did his father, Finn McCool, possess?

Convinced that he could not win a duel against such a formidable rival, Benandonner excused himself, his pride overshadowed by a newfound respect and fear. He hurried back to Scotland, and while doing so, he desperately dismantled the causeway behind him, eager to put distance between himself and the mighty Finn. The remnants of that causeway, now known as the Giant's Causeway in Ireland and Fingal's Cave in Scotland, are said to be proof of this legendary encounter.

The Giant's Causeway, Northern Ireland.
code poet on Flickr., CC BY-SA 2.0 <https://creativecommons.org/licenses/by-sa/2.0>, via Wikimedia Commons: https://commons.wikimedia.org/wiki/File:Causeway-code_poet-4.jpg

Fingal's Cave, Scotland.

The Isle of Skye

The Isle of Skye is yet another treasure trove for Scottish myths and legends. With its rugged cliffs, the Isle of Skye is a land where the boundary between reality and legend blurs. Among its many enthralling tales, the story of the Old Man of Storr stands tall—quite literally—as one of the isle's most captivating legends. There are a few tales that tell the story of this magnificent and towering rock formation. The shortest tale tells us that this striking pinnacle is the remains of a giant. Centuries ago, the isle was said to have been a home for giants. However, war constantly raged across the land, and during one particular battle, an unnamed giant fell on the Trotternish Peninsula. For unknown reasons, his body was abandoned, but instead of the body decaying, the land swallowed it up, leaving only one part of the giant protruding from the ground. While some say the Old Man of Storr was the fallen giant's thumb, others suggest it was a rather more intimate part of his lower body.

The Old Man of Storr, Isle of Skye.

Another story attributes the mystical landscape of Skye to the isle's mischievous fairies. The tale revolves around a local couple known for their devotion to each other. Every day, without fail, they climbed the hills of Skye and sat there, witnessing the beauty that Mother Nature holds. However, as the years turned to decades, the couple aged, and the climb grew more challenging. Eventually, the wife, with her strength waning, could no longer make the journey. Her husband, on the other hand, was steadfast in their tradition. Without complaint, he carried her on his back, determined to keep their ritual alive.

As more time passed, even the husband's strength began to dwindle, but his resolve never wavered. The mysterious fairies of Skye, having observed this display of love and tenacity, were moved and intrigued. They appeared before the couple, offering to grant the husband's silent wish that his wife could accompany him wherever he went.

With a heart full of love and hope, the husband carried his wife up the hill one last time. Upon reaching the summit, the fairies, true to their word but not without their own brand of mischief, transformed the couple into a massive stone pillar. United in stone, the couple would forever be together, an eternal symbol of love and dedication.

Not all of Skye's tales are tinged with the fairies' trickery. One such story is of a kind-hearted farmer who lived at the foot of these same mystical slopes. This farmer, known for his generosity and good nature, one day happened upon a Brownie in distress. Brownies, according to Scottish lore, are benevolent household spirits known to aid in domestic tasks under the cover of night. In this particular tale, the Brownie appeared to be injured. So, without hesitation, the farmer offered shelter and care.

Grateful for the farmer's kindness, the Brownie promised to repay his benevolence. True to its word, the Brownie became the farmer's unseen helper. Night after night, the farmer awoke to find his chores completed and his fields tended to with great precision and care.

The farmer's fortunes grew, as did his gratitude toward his unseen helper. Since he did not wish for free labor, the farmer often left out small tokens of appreciation, such as bowls of fresh cream or freshly baked bread, all of which would be gone by morning. Their friendship grew closer each year until tragedy hit.

The farmer was engulfed with sadness when his beloved wife suddenly passed away after battling a terminal disease. His heart shattered to pieces, and he was so heartbroken that he died the next day. The Brownie was devastated upon hearing news of its dear friend's death. In a display of appreciation and honor, the creature carved out a memorial to forever remember the kind-hearted farmer, creating the world-famous Old Man of Storr.

Chapter 2: Legendary Heroes and Warriors

Much like the epic tales of Herakles in Greek mythology or the heroic deeds of Aeneas in Roman lore, Scottish legends of heroes like William Wallace and Robert the Bruce resonate deeply with the ethos of their people. These stories, rich in not only drama but also moral lessons, served as a guide for the Scots, who had to wade through some pretty turbulent periods in history. These characters, born from a blend of history and myth, have transcended their mortal origins to become symbols of national pride. Their stories are far more than mere entertainment; they are the bedrock upon which the Scottish nation has been shaped and defined.

Sir William Wallace is a popular national hero of Scotland. His story, set against the backdrop of English domination over Scottish lands, is a saga of resistance, valor, and sacrifice. The late 13th and early 14th centuries saw Scotland under increasing pressure from the English Crown, which sought to assert control over its northern neighbor. This period of political turmoil and unrest laid the foundation for Wallace's emergence as a pivotal figure in Scotland's struggle for freedom.

Stained glass featuring a depiction of Sir William Wallace.

Born around 1270, Wallace grew up in Scotland, where the shadow of English rule loomed large. His early life, shrouded in the mists of time, is a blend of fact and folklore. It is believed that he was the son of a Scottish landowner, possibly a minor noble. His youth was marked by a growing resentment against presence and influence of the English in Scotland.

The flame of rebellion was ignited in Wallace's heart when he witnessed a series of injustices. The spark that set his path ablaze was an encounter with English soldiers in the town of Lanark. There are few details about the incident, but according to legend, Wallace was incensed by the unjust killing of his beloved, Marion Braidfute. He retaliated by killing William Heselrig, the English sheriff of the town. This act of defiance marked the beginning of Wallace's legendary resistance against English rule.

His exceptional leadership skills and military acumen shone even brighter on the morning of September 11th, 1297. Standing atop a high hill, William Wallace looked out over the River Forth, his eyes blazing with the fire of impending battle. Those who saw his presence at the time likely thought that he was a striking figure, full of energy and charisma, and that he was more than prepared for the upcoming bloodshed. Below him was the narrow wooden Stirling Bridge stretching across the river; this was the location where one of Scotland's most famous fights would take place.

When the time drew near, Wallace eyed the movement of his enemies on the other side of the battlefield. Next to him were his loyal Scottish troops, a diverse group including farmers, blacksmiths, and some lower-ranking nobles lined up in a somewhat disorganized formation. Their eyes, filled with a mix of fear and determination, were all trained on their leader, awaiting his command. Wallace's army was outmatched in numbers and equipment, but their strong resilience and spirit would drive them to achieve success.

The Stirling Bridge today.
https://commons.wikimedia.org/wiki/File:Stirling_Bridge.jpg

On the other side, one could witness a sea of English soldiers, led by the earl of Surrey and Hugh de Cressingham, making an advance. The troops were filled with well-equipped knights and soldiers, were well versed in vicious battles, and were so used to winning that they thought the Scots to be nothing but mere disturbances. As they approached the bridge, one could hear the loud sounds of their armor clanking, their horses neighing continuously, and the piercing shouts of English soldiers. They were confident they would emerge victorious that day. Little did they know they were heading straight into a trap.

As the first units of the English army began to cross the narrow bridge, Wallace's strategic genius became apparent. He had allowed just enough of the enemy to cross, creating a bottleneck. With a thunderous roar that seemed to shake the very earth, Wallace led his men in a ferocious charge. The Scots, fueled by a fervent desire for freedom, descended upon the trapped English with a ferocity that belied their humble origins.

The narrow bridge became a scene of chaos, the clash of steel on steel resounding along the waterfront. Wallace wielded his sword with lethal grace, cutting down English soldiers with each swing. His fellow Scots, emboldened by their leader's valor, fought with a wild, untamed ferocity, their battle cries merging with the sounds of battle to create a symphony of carnage.

As more English troops tried to cross the bridge, the congestion turned their advance into a death march. The Scottish forces seized the opportunity and pushed back with renewed vigor. The river, once a serene ribbon of blue, turned crimson with the blood of fallen soldiers.

Amidst the chaos, Wallace stood as a symbol of indomitable will. His presence on the battlefield was electrifying. He inspired his men to feats of bravery that would have seemed impossible. Under his leadership, the Scots turned the tide against their oppressors, transforming their disadvantage into a weapon. As the battle reached its climax, the English were completely thrown into disarray. Sensing victory, the Scots pressed harder, driving their enemies back across the bridge.

In the aftermath, as the sun set over a battlefield strewn with the dead and dying, Wallace stood triumphant, his sword dripping with the blood of his foes. The Battle of Stirling Bridge was not just a military victory; it was also a declaration, a statement of Scottish resilience and courage. This victory sent shockwaves throughout England and established Wallace as a symbol of Scottish defiance.

Following this triumph, Wallace was appointed as "Guardian of Scotland," a position that gave him considerable authority. Yet, the

English were not easily deterred. A year after the stunning defeat at Stirling Bridge, on July 22nd, 1298, the stage was set for another epic clash: the Battle of Falkirk.

Wallace surveyed the battlefield with a sharp eye. He had chosen his ground carefully, positioning his seasoned warriors and raw recruits on a broad plain near Falkirk. The Scottish spearmen, who were arranged in close-knit formations called schiltrons, were like a thorny hedge against the English cavalry. However, unlike the Battle of Stirling Bridge, Wallace and his forces were up against a tougher opponent. They had to face the English army, led by King Edward I. It was made up of heavy cavalry and seasoned archers who were determined to put an end to the Scottish uprising.

The ground trembled beneath the thunderous charge of the English cavalry. The air was filled with the deadly whistling of arrows when the famed English longbowmen, a lethal addition to Edward's arsenal, unleashed their volleys. The Scottish schiltrons, though formidable against cavalry, were vulnerable to this rain of death.

Wallace was undaunted, though. He rallied his men, his voice cutting through the chaos. As a figure of hope amidst despair, he moved through the ranks, urging his men to hold their ground. For a time, the Scottish formations held firm, their pikes repelling the fierce charges of the English knights. However, the relentless barrage of arrows took its toll, as the deadly shafts accurately found their mark, piercing armor and flesh.

The battle soon turned into a maelstrom of violence and bloodshed. The English cavalry exploited the gaps opened by the archers and charged into the heart of the Scottish ranks. The schiltrons began to buckle and break under the unyielding pressure. Wallace fought bravely, his sword moving quickly as he tried to hold back the enemy, but the odds were stacked against him.

As the sun dipped low, casting long shadows over the field of Falkirk, the battle drew to its grim conclusion. The Scottish army was routed, their lines shattered, leaving the field littered with the bloodied bodies of the fallen. Wallace was forced to flee.

The Battle of Falkirk was a devastating blow to the Scottish cause, and it was a bitter lesson in the cruelty of war. Wallace's military career never fully recovered from this setback. Despite the loss, Wallace's spirit remained unbroken. He continued to fight for Scottish independence, though his tactics shifted more toward guerrilla warfare. However, his resistance came to an end in 1305 when he was betrayed and captured by the English.

Wallace's trial and execution in London were designed to be a spectacle of English power and a warning to other would-be rebels. After being convicted of high treason, he was subjected to the most horrific execution of the medieval era. He was dragged naked behind a horse to the location of his execution. He was then hung and emasculated while still breathing. His private parts were burned before his eyes. Only then did the executioner cut him open and quartered his lifeless body. The four parts were transported to Newcastle, Berwick, Perth, and Stirling to be publicly displayed.

A depiction of Wallace's trial in Westminster Hall.

Wallace became an immortal symbol of Scotland's struggle for freedom. His name became synonymous with resistance against oppression, and his story was a rallying cry for those who valued liberty over life. The brutal manner of his death only further cemented his status as a martyr for Scottish independence.

Over the centuries, the legend of William Wallace grew, with his life and deeds taking on mythic proportions. He became not just a historical figure but also a symbol of national identity, embodying the resilience, courage, and undying spirit of the Scottish people. His story, immortalized in ballads, literature, and even in iconic films like *Braveheart*, continues to inspire and resonate with Scots and freedom-lovers around the world.

Robert the Bruce

While the sun set on the Battle of Falkirk, a new dawn was quietly rising in the form of another hero, Robert the Bruce. Born into the aristocracy on July 11th, 1274, his early life was filled with noble duties and court intrigues, which was a stark contrast to Wallace's humble upbringing. The young Robert grew up in a Scotland torn apart by the strife of the First War of Scottish Independence. This challenging environment shaped him, mixing his sense of loyalty and ambition with a strong desire for freedom.

Robert, with his sharp mind and charming personality, navigated through the treacherous waters of Scottish politics with a deft hand. Initially, he chose to show his allegiance to King Edward I of England, but this was nothing but a decision based on practicality. Deep down, Robert the Bruce was a true Scotsman who had an undying love for his homeland. This inner struggle defined much of his early life as he wrestled with his role in the ongoing struggle for Scotland's independence.

The turning point for Robert came with the death of Wallace. In 1306, in a bold move, Robert the Bruce claimed the Scottish crown. His coronation was a defiant proclamation of Scotland's enduring spirit. However, his path to the throne was not without peril. The English viewed his coronation as an act of treachery and intensified their efforts to subdue Scotland.

Robert the Bruce crowned as the king of the Scots.

Robert's early reign was marked by a series of setbacks and defeats. He was forced into hiding. His forces were scattered, and his kingdom was in disarray. However, these tough times only made him more determined. From the shadows, he waged a guerrilla war against the English, using clever and unexpected strategies. Slowly, he regained strength, rallying the Scottish clans to his cause.

The culmination of Robert's struggle came in the summer of 1314 at the Battle of Bannockburn. The English, led by Edward II, sought to crush the Scottish rebellion once and for all. They marched north with a massive army, confident in their numbers and might. But Robert the Bruce, ever the strategist, picked the perfect spot for the battle. Near the Bannock Burn (a stream to the southwest of Stirling), he prepared his forces. These men had been toughened by years of unrest and fighting, and they were ready for the chance to fight once more for their freedom.

As the English approached, the vastly outnumbered Scottish army braced for the assault. Robert the Bruce, astride his horse, spoke to his men, calling them to arms. The battle commenced with the Scots employing tight schiltrons, their spears serving as a death sentence for the English cavalry. Robert led from the front. He was a whirlwind in battle, his prowess and leadership turning the tide.

The English became bogged down by the marshy ground and were taken aback by the intensity of the Scottish defense. They began to falter. Seeing their chance, the Scottish army launched a powerful counterattack, believing in their imminent victory. The English lines crumbled, turning their orderly retreat into a panicked flight. Bannockburn turned out to be a tremendous win for the Scots, showcasing Robert the Bruce's leadership skills and the indomitable spirit of his people.

The aftermath of Bannockburn was a turning point in the war. Scotland's independence was effectively secured, though skirmishes and political struggles would continue. Robert the Bruce's reign, post-Bannockburn, was marked by efforts to consolidate his kingdom and secure Scotland's future. He worked tirelessly to strengthen his realm, seeking diplomatic recognition and stability for his people.

In his later years, Robert the Bruce's health began to deteriorate. Yet, his determination and dedication to Scotland never declined. He passed away on June 7th, 1329, but his impact went far beyond his lifetime. Under his leadership, Scotland became a reborn nation.

Robert the Bruce, much like William Wallace before him, became a legend in Scotland. His life and actions became a key part of what it means to be a proud Scot today. His story continues to inspire new generations.

Black Agnes

Scotland also witnessed a woman with incredible determination and an unbreakable spirit come to the forefront. This female figure made such a strong impact that her name is now immortalized in Scottish history.

An illustration of Black Agnes from a children's storybook published in 1906.
https://commons.wikimedia.org/wiki/File:Black_Agnes,_from_a_children%27s_history_book.jpg

Agnes Randolph, Countess of Dunbar and March, was nicknamed "Black Agnes" due to her distinctive dark hair and eyes. As the lady of Dunbar Castle, she was in charge of protecting the fortress, which was located in a crucial position near the southeastern coast of Scotland. Her moment of legend came in 1338 when William Montagu, the 1st Earl of Salisbury, and his formidable English army laid siege to Dunbar Castle. Montagu was undeniably an experienced leader, but his constant victories sometimes blurred his assumptions. Since the castle was under a woman's leadership, he thought it would be easy to capture. Little did he know that he would meet a foe as unyielding as the very stones of Dunbar itself.

The siege began with a traditional display of might: a volley of rocks hurled by trebuchets. This tactic was designed to shatter both the walls and the people's resolve. But Agnes wasn't fazed by this attack. In a bold move, she had her maids wipe down the castle battlements with handkerchiefs, a gesture of contempt that angered Montagu and his soldiers.

As the days stretched into weeks, the English laid relentless assaults against the castle's defenses. Yet, under Agnes's command, the garrison fought back with a tenacity that belied their small numbers. In one of the siege's most dramatic moments, Montagu captured Agnes's brother, John Randolph, 3ʳᵈ Earl of Moray, and threatened to execute him before the castle walls. Agnes retorted that his death would only make her the heir to their family's land. Eventually, her brother was spared. It was not done out of mercy but because the English realized their threat possessed no power over her iron will.

Throughout the siege, Agnes's leadership was a source of inspiration for her people. Her wit, courage, and relentless defiance were key to keeping the castle's defense strong. She rallied her troops, uplifted her subjects, and, according to legend, even taunted her enemies with insults, further inflaming their frustration.

What remains of Dunbar Castle today.

After five long months, the siege of Dunbar Castle ended not with a bang but with a whimper. The weary and demoralized English gave up. They lifted the siege and retreated, their spirits crushed by the weight of Agnes's otherworldly resistance. Agnes's name, "Black Agnes of Dunbar," echoed through Scottish history as a symbol of the strong resistance and undaunted courage of Scotland's daughters.

These legendary figures have become etched into the very soul of Scotland. They are not figments of imagination or relics of a bygone era. They are living, breathing presences in the Scottish consciousness.

Their stories carry a deep sense of meaning. They were shared over and over again, not only for fun around the fireplace but also to teach each new generation about their identity and to instill pride in them. Just as the Greek epics taught lessons of heroism and the Roman tales spoke of civic duty and empire, the Scottish legends served as a compass, guiding the Scots to stay true to their cultural and national values.

Chapter 3: Deities and Spirits: The Pantheon of Scottish Mythology

The stories of the Irish gods are particularly striking, each one equipped with colorful journeys. These stories were not just limited to the vast lands of Ireland; they spread far and wide, finding a special place in the hearts of the Scottish people as well. Among these gods, Lugh, known for his grandeur and strength, held an important role in both Irish and Scottish mythologies.

Our tale begins in an age when the world was young, and the lands of Ireland lay under the shadow of the Fomorians. This ancient race, believed to be from under the sea or the underworld, was as formidable as they were fearsome. Descriptions of them vary, with some accounts depicting them with the grotesque heads of goats and bodies created from the very elements of chaos. They were the embodiment of destructive natural forces. Scholars believe their appearance symbolizes the untamed and wild aspects of nature.

Depiction of the Fomorians.
https://commons.wikimedia.org/wiki/File:The_Fomorians,_Duncan_1912.jpg

At the helm of this race was Balor of the Baleful Eye, a king whose very gaze wrought destruction. When Balor's eye was opened, it could scorch the earth and lay waste to entire armies. Under his reign, the Fomorians brought unspeakable chaos upon the land, waging wars and enslaving peoples. Their most relentless adversaries were the Tuatha Dé Danann, a race of deities and skilled warriors. The ongoing conflict between the Fomorians and the Tuatha Dé Danann was fueled by land disagreements and deep-rooted hostilities.

The Tuatha Dé Danann as depicted in John Duncan's *The Riders of the Sidhe* (1911).
https://commons.wikimedia.org/wiki/File:Riders_of_th_Sidhe_(big).jpg

However, there was a prophecy that terrified Balor. This prophecy foretold his doom at the hands of his own grandson. To prevent this from coming true, Balor locked his daughter, Ethniu, in a tower of crystal, away from the world of men.

But destiny always has a way of fulfilling itself. Despite his efforts to change his fate, the world saw the birth of Lugh, who was predicted to take his grandfather's life. Lugh's hair looked like spun gold, and his eyes mirrored the ocean's depths. He was a stark contrast to Balor. He was a figure who inspired both awe and admiration. Lugh was known for his many talents. He was an artist, a powerful warrior, and a wise being. His heritage was a mix of the divine and mortal, combining the lineage of both the Fomorians and the Tuatha Dé Danann.

Lugh's journey eventually led him to the Hill of Tara, the seat of the Tuatha Dé Danann's king, Nuada. His attempt to join Nuada's court was initially met with resistance. The doorkeeper refused to let him in, claiming that the court already had experts in each skill Lugh claimed to have. Lugh then pointed out that no one had all his skills, which was what got him inside. Just as he expected, his versatility impressed Nuada, who saw in Lugh the potential to lead the Tuatha Dé Danann to victory against their oppressors.

Lugh's arrival at the court was a turning point. He triumphed over the king's champion and deity, Ogma, in a contest of strength and entertained the court with his harp playing. As time passed, Lugh noticed how the Tuatha Dé Danann were slowly accepting their fate. Not fond of the fact that the Fomorians held the higher ground, Lugh pledged to guide them to liberation. Nuada recognized Lugh's leadership and skill and appointed him as the commander of the Tuatha Dé Danann.

So, the stage was set for the legendary Battle of Mag Tuireadh. Lugh, who led the fight, was unstoppable, wielding his spear and sling with lethal accuracy. The battle was fierce, filled with clashing swords and magical powers. Unfortunately, King Nuada met his end during this intense fight. He was slain by the evil Balor.

The battle reached its peak in a fateful showdown. Lugh finally confronted his grandfather, Balor, in a duel that was about more than just physical strength; it was also a battle of fate and will. With cunning and skill, Lugh managed to turn Balor's destructive gaze upon himself by hitting his grandfather's eye with his sling. This act fulfilled the prophecy. Balor was defeated, and with his fall, the Fomorians' reign of terror ended.

The conclusion of the battle marked a new era for Ireland. The land began to thrive under the Tuatha Dé Danann's care. Lugh's victory freed the land from turmoil and disorder. The details of Lugh's final days remain shrouded in mystery. Some tales speak of a tragic demise at the hands of his own kin, a fate all too common among the gods. Others believe he simply faded from the world, his spirit becoming one with the very lands he fought to protect.

Lugh's influence lives on in the myths and legends of Ireland and Scotland. His story continues to enchant people, showing the lasting impact of myths and the timeless stories of ancient gods and heroes.

Bridie

Bridie, often likened to the Irish goddess Brigid, reigns as a deity of profound grace and nurturing power. Her essence, deeply rooted in the cycle of the seasons, manifests as the guardian of healing, childbirth, and the harbinger of spring. In Bridie's presence, the land awakens, and life blooms anew with the promise of renewal and growth.

Bridie's appearance, a blend of gentleness and formidable strength, mirrors the nurturing essence of the earth. Her hair, shining like the golden light of early morning, and her eyes, serene as tranquil waters, symbolize her deep connection to the rebirth of life. Dressed in robes that sparkle with the bright palettes of spring, Bridie was believed to walk through the green meadows and woods, leaving in her wake a trail of blossoming flora and revived life.

In both Scottish and Irish folktales, Bridie's tales resonate with the miracle of healing and the rejuvenation of the land after winter's cold embrace. Revered as the protector of livestock and the guardian of fertility, people often called on her in difficult times, hoping for her help to make their crops and animals thrive. Her festival, Imbolc, marks the beginning of spring. It's a time of celebration and renewal where her followers come together around holy fires to pay tribute to her ability to bring change and create new life.

One particular tale recounts Bridie's evolution from a pagan goddess to a revered Christian saint. This tale blends elements of myth, history, and spiritual change. It takes place during a time when Scotland's religious beliefs were evolving. In the story, Bridie's sacred flame, which was once lit in her honor in old forests, and her wells and springs, which were known for healing the sick, find a new place in Christian monasteries. Her monastery at Kildare, for one, became a center of learning and healing.

There, her sacred flame burns continuously and is tended by her devoted nuns.

An illustration of Bridie or Brigid.
https://commons.wikimedia.org/wiki/File:Thecomingofbrideduncan1917.jpg

This story also delves into the miraculous feats associated with Saint Brigid, each echoing Bridie's ancient powers. From healing the sick to the miraculous multiplication of food, Saint Brigid's acts are a reflection of Bridie's divine qualities and influence. The narrative draws parallels between Bridie's role in heralding spring and Saint Brigid's celebration on February 1ˢᵗ, the day marking the beginning of spring in the Christian calendar. This story of transformation and endurance reflects the enduring nature of myths and the adaptability of divine figures through changing eras. Bridie, in her transition to Saint Brigid, became a bridge between the old and the new world.

Other tales highlight Saint Brigid's miraculous deeds, such as her cloak expanding to claim land for her monastery and her ability to turn water into beer to feed the poor. These miracles, while rooted in Christian lore, echo Bridie's ancient connection to the land and her power to nourish and protect.

Stained glass featuring Saint Brigid.
Octave 444, CC BY-SA 4.0 <https://creativecommons.org/licenses/by-sa/4.0>, via Wikimedia Commons: https://commons.wikimedia.org/wiki/File:Sainte_Brigitte_%C3%A9glise_Macon.jpg

Cernunnos

Cernunnos is known as a deity whose presence is strongly felt in the ancient Celtic lands, including the mystical realms of Scotland. This enigmatic figure, with the majesty of a god yet the mystery of the untamed wilds, is a mediator between man and nature. He was believed to be a silent guardian of the forests and their creatures.

The deity is often depicted with the antlers of a stag, which scholars suggest embodies the primal power and grace of nature. His appearance, a blend of human and beast, symbolizes his deep connection with all living things. He is often shown seated in a lordly pose, antlers rising proudly from his head. His wise and deep gaze seems to transcend time, holding within it the secrets of the ancient and mysterious woods.

The history of Cernunnos is shrouded in the mists of time, with only fragments of his story surviving. Researchers suggest he was a god of fertility, wealth, and the underworld, but a lot about him is still unclear. The Pillar of the Boatmen, an ancient artifact, gives us one of the few images of Cernunnos. Another striking depiction of this horned god is found on the Gundestrup Cauldron, believed to date back to 200 BCE. Here, he is shown in majestic splendor, adorned with torcs and surrounded by animals, perhaps highlighting his role as a master of beasts. He was seen as a ruler who could bring predator and prey together in harmony.

A depiction of an antlered deity, possibly Cernunnos, on the Gundestrup Cauldron.

Despite his compelling image, Cernunnos remains a figure of mystery. There are no myths or legends directly tied to his name. Some scholars believe Shakespeare's character Herne the Hunter might be based on Cernunnos. In Shakespeare's portrayal, Herne is a ghostly hunter who haunts Windsor Forest. The tale goes that Herne was a keeper of the forest favored by King Richard II, who admired his hunting skills. However, Herne's story takes a tragic turn when he gains the jealousy of the other hunters.

One day, while on a hunt, the king was attacked by a stag. Herne courageously intervened, saving the king, although he ended up mortally wounded himself. As he lay dying, a mysterious figure, often interpreted as a wizard or dark magician, appeared before him. He offered to save Herne's life on one condition: the famed hunter must give up his hunting skills. Desperate and not prepared to proceed to the afterlife, Herne agreed. And so, he miraculously recovered, but as promised, he lost his prowess in hunting.

Shunned and disgraced, Herne was driven to despair. In his anguish, he ventured into the forest. He attached his antlered helmet to a tree and took his own life. Because of this, legend says that Herne's spirit was doomed to haunt Windsor Forest. He was often depicted riding a horse and wearing antlers on his head. He was accompanied by the sounds of howling hounds and a wild hunt. His appearance was considered an omen of bad luck or misfortune.

However, the story of Herne the Hunter has evolved over the centuries. Some versions suggest that his spirit was actually a protector of the forest, though there are others that portray him as a malevolent entity. Theories about his origins range from him being an ancient pagan deity to a later invention by Shakespeare. The connection to Cernunnos is drawn from the shared imagery of antlers and mastery over animals, but it remains a topic of debate among scholars.

The possible link between Cernunnos and Saint Ciarán further blurs the line between pagan deities and Christian saints, suggesting a continuity and adaptation of ancient beliefs into the Christian era. This connection, while tenuous, speaks to the enduring presence of Cernunnos in the cultural and spiritual landscape of the Celts.

Despite the scant details and the lack of surviving stories, Cernunnos has not faded into obscurity. Instead, he has been reborn in the realms of pop culture and modern pagan practice. His powerful and mysterious image continues to captivate the imagination, a reminder of a time when gods walked in the deep forests and whispered in the winds.

Angus

Angus Og, known as Aonghas Òg in Scotland and Oengus in Ireland, was a deity famed for his remarkable allure and complexity. He exudes the vibrancy of youth and the allure of love, making him a central figure in many stories. With his golden hair that mirrored the sun's brilliance and eyes that reflected the depth of the deepest lochs, Angus Og was the embodiment of beauty and youthful vigor.

In Scottish folklore, Angus Og was celebrated as the handsome son of the mighty Cailleach, who reigned over the harsh and biting winter months. This deity of youth hid in the enchanted realm of Tír na nÓg, where time stood still and age was but a distant memory. Here, in this land of everlasting youth, Angus spent the winter waiting for a sign that heralded the coming of spring.

One such dream came to him in the heart of winter. He dreamed of Bridie, who appeared as a maiden so beautiful that her very existence signaled the renewal of the earth and the awakening of all life; some suggest that Bridie and the goddess Brigid were the same figure. However, this dream was marred by a cruel reality. Bridie was imprisoned by the Cailleach, who was envious of her brilliance and beauty. The divine winter hag was intent on delaying the arrival of spring and did so by giving Bridie endless, impossible tasks. Her goal was to weaken Bridie's luminous presence, which threatened to end her own cold and dark rule.

Driven by love and the desire to restore balance to the seasons, Angus Og borrowed three days of warmth from August. Mounted on his white steed, the god of youth journeyed forth, piercing through the cold of winter. It was a race against both time and the unyielding grip of the Cailleach. His quest, spanning the breadth of the land, eventually led him to the winter hag's underground palace just as the first hints of spring were beginning to stir the world from its winter slumber.

The meeting between the two beautiful beings in the depths of the Cailleach's underground realm was a moment of awakening and change. When Angus's and Bridie's eyes met, the earth responded. Flowers burst into bloom, the grass turned lush green, and the air itself seemed to sing with the promise of life. Bridie, previously dressed in shabby clothes, now glowed in white robes adorned with silver and embellished with the first blooms of spring and summer. Their union, marked by a grand wedding ceremony, symbolized the triumph of love over the desolation of winter.

Yet, this moment of joy was fleeting, as the Cailleach, enraged by the disruption of her reign, chased them with storms and tempests. Mounted on her dark steed, the Cailleach was a harbinger of winter's lingering fury. The land was immediately caught in a battle of seasons. However, time was not on the divine hag's side, as her power began to wane. As she retreated to the Well of Youth for rejuvenation, her strength greatly diminished, she succumbed to a deep slumber. In her absence, Angus and Bridie ascended as the King and Queen of Summer, heralding a time of warmth, growth, and bountiful joy.

Blue Men of the Minch

In a time long past, as the Scottish sun slowly sank below the horizon, a small ship called the *Sea Whisperer* set sail from the rugged coasts of the Outer Hebrides, right off the west coast of mainland Scotland. Its crew, toughened by the salt and spray of many voyages, were bound for faraway lands, their hearts filled with the promise of adventure and the allure of the unknown.

The captain of the ship, a robust man with sun-bleached hair, steered his vessel with a steady hand. His crew, a mix of old friends and young lads, was eager to prove its worth. They worked together harmoniously, their laughter and songs mingling with the sounds of the ocean and the ship's gentle creaking.

As they ventured farther into the deep waters, a hush fell over the *Sea Whisperer*. The seasoned sailors knew they were nearing the Minch, a stretch of water whispered about in taverns and harbors. This was believed to be the home of the Na Fir Ghorma or the Blue Men of the Minch. Legends spoke of these creatures, saying they were beings who looked much like men save for their blue skin.

The Blue Men, it was said, were masters of the sea, capable of conjuring storms with a flick of their hand. In calm weather, they would drift, half-submerged and in a slumber as peaceful as the still sea. These creatures swam with their torsos above the water, moving with the elegance of friendly dolphins. Their eyes were said to gleam with the knowledge of age-old ocean tides and the secret of the sea's depths.

The captain, with both of his weathered hands firmly wrapped around the helm, kept a watchful eye for any peculiar signs coming from the ocean. According to legends and tales, if the Blue Men approached, their chief would present a challenge—a duel of wit and poetry. Failing to respond to their riddles could lead to catastrophe and unleash the fury of the deep sea itself.

As twilight deepened, an eerie stillness settled upon the waters. The crew grew silent as they felt the sudden change in the atmosphere. And then, as if conjured by their own thoughts, the Blue Men appeared. Their blue skin shimmered under the fading light, and their keen eyes, sharp as the horizon line, focused on the *Sea Whisperer*.

The chief of the Blue Men soon emerged, displaying his imposing figure to the wary sailors. His deep and resonant voice echoed across the waves, bouncing off the ship's hull. He shouted the first two lines of a cryptic verse, issuing his challenge directly to the captain:

"In the depths where shadows play,

Where the light of day fades away..."

The crew held their breath, their eyes locked on their captain, who stood firm at the helm. His mind raced, the lines of the verse turning in his head. He was well aware that the fate of the *Sea Whisperer* and her crew hung in the balance. Then, with a voice as steady as the North Star, the determined captain shouted back the completing lines of the verse:

"...We guard the secrets old and deep,

In the ocean's heart, where dreams do sleep."

It was as if the sea was holding its breath in anticipation. Then, the chief of the Blue Men burst into laughter, a sound almost resembling the rolling of distant thunder. This laughter was not to mock; instead, it was a sign of respect, a recognition of the captain's wit and worth. With just a simple nod, the Blue Men dove beneath the waves, plunging back into the depths, vanishing as swiftly as they had come.

The crew of the *Sea Whisperer* breathed a sigh of relief, thankful for their captain's quick thinking and for sparing them from the unpredictable wrath of the sea. The captain, with a grin as wide as the horizon, turned to his crew, his eyes sparkling with the thrill of the encounter.

"Tonight, we drink to the Blue Men," he announced. "To their riddles and the secrets of the ocean!"

The tale of their encounter with the Na Fir Ghorma became a legend, a story told in hushed tones around warm fires and over clinking beer mugs. This tale of the sea and its ancient inhabitants reminded everyone of the respect due to the ocean's mysteries.

Chapter 4: The Fae and the Underworld: Different Realms

We are never alone in the world. The universe is full of mystery, and nowhere is this more evident than in the heart of Scotland. According to old beliefs, here, among the blooming thistles and mist-covered hills, existed a world parallel to ours—a realm steeped in magic and mystery. This was the world of the Fae.

The Fae, or fairies, are not just figments of imagination; they are integral to Scottish mythology. They embody the essence of the land, the whisper of the wind through the heather, and the rustle of leaves in the ancient forests. The Fae exist in a realm that overlaps with our world but remains just out of sight, with some claiming it was accessible through ancient hills, hidden paths, or within the heart of wild places.

Some of the most well known of these beings are the inhabitants of the Seelie and Unseelie Courts. The Seelie Court, sometimes known as the "Blessed Ones," is often depicted as a procession of brilliant light gliding through the night air. These fairies love music and dancing, and they are known for their magnificent parties and celebrations under the serene, moonlit sky. These fairies are most active during nighttime, and more than often, their journeys are not just for fun; they often help those in need. The Seelie are very fond of humans, and while they are prone to mischief, especially when boredom strikes, their pranks are usually harmless, a reflection of their generally benevolent nature toward mankind.

The Code of the Seelie Court is a set of principles that govern the behavior of its members. This code emphasizes the following:

1. **Honor Above All:** For the Seelie, their honor is their most treasured possession. It is even more important than life. A Seelie would rather face death than endure the shame of dishonor, and they strive to never bring disgrace upon their kin.

2. **Love Conquers All:** The Seelie hold love in the highest regard, seeing it as the purest expression of the soul. While romantic love is esteemed the most, they also value strong friendships and non-romantic relationships.

3. **Beauty Is Life:** For the Seelie, beauty is paramount. They are naturally attracted to all forms of beauty and are willing to fight to preserve it, whether it's a person, a place, or an object.

4. **Never Forget a Debt:** The Seelie take debts seriously. They are committed to repaying them, whether they are favors or slights. They believe in repaying kindness promptly and seeking justice quickly for any wrongs done to them.

The Unseelie Court, on the other hand, is a darker assembly. Known as the "Unblessed Ones," they present a stark contrast to their Seelie counterparts. They are often envisioned as a dark cloud sweeping across the sky, their unnerving laughter and howls carrying on the wind. The Unseelie Fae are often described as less human in appearance, with wild, untamed features that reflect their more nefarious nature. Some are said to have glowing red eyes, sharp teeth, and claws, a stark contrast to the luminescent beauty of the Seelie Court.

While some suggest the Unseelie are not inherently evil, it is safe to assume that they are far from kind. They lean toward malevolence and often seek to harm or deceive humans. According to Scottish myths, they are sometimes portrayed as fallen Seelie who failed to meet the Seelie Court's strict standards of chivalry. As a result, the Unseelie Court became a haven for these outcasts, as well as for enslaved mortals and various monstrous creatures.

The Code of the Unseelie Court reflects their darker nature and consists of the following:

1. **Embracing Change:** The Unseelie embraces chaos, viewing stability as an illusion. They believe in adapting and evolving to thrive in a world that is always changing.

2. **Glamor is Free:** Glamor is a natural magic of the Daoine Sidhe or the Fae. It can be used to create illusions or cast enchantments. This natural magic is a favorite tool of the Unseelie. Unlike the more cautious Seelie, the Unseelie use this power without any hesitation, believing that any power not utilized is essentially wasted.

3. **Honor Is a Lie:** The Unseelie dismisses the idea of honor, focusing on self-interest instead. They find truth in self-pursuit rather than in meeting obligations to others.

4. **Prioritizing Passion:** For the Unseelie, living passionately is the most authentic way of life. They act on their instincts and desires, often ignoring duties or the repercussions of their actions.

The abilities of these fairies are as varied as their appearances. Some have the power to shape-shift, taking on forms of animals or even humans. Others wield magic that can either bless or curse and heal or harm. The Fae are also known for their skill in illusion. They are able to create glamors that can make the old appear young, the mundane seem magnificent, or even make themselves invisible to human eyes.

In Scottish folklore, encounters with the Fae are often cautionary tales. One such story tells of a young man who, on his way home, heard the enchanting music of a fairy celebration. Drawn by the melody, he found himself in the presence of the Seelie Court. He joined their dance, and when he finally left, he discovered that what felt like hours was actually years. Everyone he knew had aged or passed away. This tale serves as a reminder of the enchanting yet perilous nature of the fairy world.

Another tale speaks of the Unseelie Court's mischief. It tells of a farmer who encountered a group of these malevolent fairies one night. They demanded his help in their mischievous deeds, and fearing their wrath, he complied. The farmer spent the night aiding the Unseelie Fae in their pranks, only to find himself cursed at dawn, unable to speak of what he saw under penalty of death. This story illustrates the darker side of the Fae and their love for chaos and trickery.

The Scots also believed in the concept of the underworld, better known as the Otherworld in their vibrant folklore. However, since the Otherworld is shrouded in mist and mystery, it stands in stark contrast to the more defined afterlives of Greek and Egyptian mythology.

In the Greek underworld, ruled by Hades, the dead embark on a final journey across the River Styx, entering a shadowy realm separated from the living. This world beneath the earth is said to be a place of souls, a realm where justice reigns in the form of rewards or punishments. Egyptian mythology also portrays an intricate afterlife, where the dead traverse through trials and judgments under the watchful eyes of Osiris, the god of the dead, in a land beyond the living.

The Scottish Otherworld is not a singular realm of the dead. It is an ethereal, parallel dimension that coexists with our world, a place where the lines between the natural and the supernatural blur. This realm is not solely for the departed; it is a mysterious domain of the Fae, a land steeped in magic and home to beings both wondrous and fearsome.

Unlike the Greek and Egyptian conceptions, the Scottish Otherworld is closely intertwined with the fairy realm. It is a place that is ever-present, hidden behind ancient hills or veiled in the mists that often blanket the Scottish landscape. It is a world where time may flow differently, where the laws of nature are mere suggestions and often ignored by the mystical beings who live there.

In Scottish folklore, certain omens or signs are not necessarily indicators of someone's impending death; instead, they may be a gateway to a more mysterious world. These omens, deeply rooted in folklore, serve as both caution and temptation, leading some to their doom and others into the depths of the unknown. Typically, strange or even terrifying creatures and spirits carry the omens and display them to mortals.

The Tale of the Bean Nighe

In a small hamlet nestled in the shadow of the Scottish Highlands lived a humble peasant named Aoidh. With calloused hands and a gentle heart, Aoidh spent his days tending to his modest farm, living a simple yet content life. However, Aoidh's peaceful existence was about to be touched by the uncanny realm of Scottish myth.

One chilly autumn evening, as the sun dipped below the rugged hills, painting the sky in shades of crimson and gold, Aoidh decided to take a shortcut home through the woods. The forest, a maze of ancient trees and whispering leaves, had always been a place of solace for him. However, that night, it held an air of mystery that made him feel the soft brushes of terror and discomfort.

As he walked, accompanied only by sounds of the crunch of leaves under his foot, Aoidh's eyes were drawn to a figure by the stream, a strange solitary woman hunched over the water. Her presence was both unexpected and unsettling at the same time. Drawing closer, Aoidh saw that she was washing clothes, her hands working tirelessly in the cold, flowing water. But it was no ordinary laundry she washed; the clothes were stained with blood, the water turning a ghostly crimson-red with each scrub.

The sight rooted Aoidh to the spot, his heart pounding with fear and a pinch of fascination. He realized, with a shiver running down his spine, that he was in the presence of the Bean Nighe, the Washing Woman of Scottish lore. It was said that the Bean Nighe was a harbinger of death, washing the blood-stained clothes of those soon to meet their end.

Torn between terror and curiosity, Aoidh found his voice.

"Why do you wash these clothes in such a place and at such an hour?" he asked, his voice barely above a whisper.

The Bean Nighe paused, her hands stilling in the water. She raised her head, and Aoidh saw her face, sorrowful yet serene, as if carrying the weight of untold secrets.

"I wash the clothes of those whose time is near," she replied, her voice almost like the rustle of leaves. "I am the omen of what is to come, the link between this world and the Otherworld."

"Am I...am I to die?" he stuttered, a tremor in his voice.

The Bean Nighe looked at him, her eyes reflecting a depth of wisdom and sorrow.

"Not you, Aoidh, but someone close to your heart. I am sorry," she said, her voice tinged with a timeless sadness.

Aoidh felt a chill that had nothing to do with the serene autumn air. He thought of his family and friends. Who among them was marked by fate? The Bean Nighe returned to her washing, the sound of the water resembling a mournful melody in the growing darkness.

As he made his way home, the encounter replayed in his mind. He knew now that the Bean Nighe was more than a myth; she was a reminder of the thin veil between life and death, a messenger from the incomprehensible Otherworld, a place of mystery and enchantment that lay just beyond the reach of the living.

In the days that followed, Aoidh's life was touched by sorrow, as the omen of the Bean Nighe came to reality. He heard news that a young woman from a nearby village had suddenly died from an unknown disease. This woman was Aoidh's first love, the one he kept close to his heart for years despite their paths having diverged long ago. Her loss left a void in Aoidh's heart.

The Tale of the Cú-Sith, the Wolf That Brings Death

In another humble village nestled among the misty rolling hills and ancient woods, an old man sat by a crackling fire, surrounded by eager, youthful faces. Among them were two young boys known for their playful mischief and boundless curiosity. The old man began to tell a tale that had been passed down through generations—the tale of the Cú-Sith and Cat Sith, mysterious creatures of Scottish folklore.

"The Cú-Sith," he began, his voice low, "is a beast of legend, a fairy dog as large as a young cow, with fur as green as the mossy hillsides. It roams the highlands and the deep valleys, its presence heralded by three blood-curdling howls." The boys leaned in closer, their eyes wide. "Those who hear these howls must find shelter before the third, for it is said that those who do not will meet a terrifying fate."

He then spoke of the Cat Sith, a large black cat with a distinctive white spot on its chest. "The Cat Sith moves like a shadow in the night, silent and watchful. Some believe it to be a transformed witch or a fairy creature, a being that steals the souls of the dead before they can journey to the next world."

One of the boys hung onto every word with a mix of fear and awe. The other boy scoffed at the story. "Just old tales to scare children," he said, a smirk on his face.

As dusk fell that day, after hours of playing in the woods, the boys started their walk home. The sky was a canvas of darkening blues and purples, and the moon hung like a silver beacon. While walking, the believing boy saw, at the corner of his eyes, a cat-like figure slowly moving through the bushes. He thought of the Cat Sith. So, he stopped and looked around, perhaps hoping he could see the cat more clearly. But the creature was nowhere to be seen; it was as if it had disappeared into thin air. Assuming it was just another cat, the boy continued walking and eventually caught up with his friend, who was already several steps ahead.

Suddenly, the stillness of the night was shattered by an eerie and otherworldly howl. The believing boy's heart skipped a beat, especially after remembering the peculiar sighting of the cat earlier. His friend, who noticed the believing boy's face turning pale, burst into laughter.

"It's just a wolf," he said, emboldened by his disbelief. "Don't tell me you believe in the story?"

Driven by a mix of curiosity and bravado, the skeptical boy ventured deeper into the woods, determined to prove the howl was nothing more than a wild animal. His friend, gripped by the stories of old, refused to follow, his steps hastening toward the safety of the village.

As the fearful boy neared the village, a second howl echoed through the woods, more chilling than the first. He saw villagers rushing to their homes, their faces etched with concern. Without hesitation, he darted home just as the third howl, a sound that seemed to carry the weight of doom, filled the air.

The boy, now safe within his home, stared out into the darkness, thoughts of his friend lingering in his mind. The night passed, and morning light broke, but the brave boy did not return. Search parties combed the woods. Their calls were answered only by their own echoes. The boy was nowhere to be found. It was as if he had vanished, as if he had been claimed by the very legends he had mocked.

The village was abuzz with whispers of the Cú-Sìth and the boy's bravery, along with the old man's story that had become a grim reality. The story of the two boys and their encounter with the unseen forces of Scottish lore became a stark reminder to all. Respect the legends and the old tales, for in the shadows of the Scottish highlands, the boundary between myth and reality is as fine as a strand of mist, and mythical beings are never too far away.

The old man would often retell the story. Each time, they seemed to gain a deeper understanding.

"Respect the legends," he would say, his voice resonating with the age-old wisdom of the land. "Our stories are more than just tales; they are echoes from an unseen world, a world much closer than you might think."

The Will-o'-the-Wisp

One late autumn evening, a daring young lad named Callum decided to explore the dense woods that bordered the village. He had grown up on tales of the will-o'-the-wisp, the flickering spirit light said to appear in the most desolate parts of the forest. The spirit was said to be responsible for the deaths of many villagers in the hilly regions of Scotland; almost everyone was told of the danger of following the will-o'-the-wisp. The spirit could not only lead unwary travelers into dense forests, full of mysteries and other unknown creatures, but it could also trick them into venturing perilously close to treacherous cliffs hidden within the dense foliage.

The will-o'-the-wisp and a snake.

The will-o'-the-wisp, known for its mysterious and deceptive glow, had a knack for leading the curious and the foolhardy to the edges of steep cliffs. Shrouded by darkness and the dense underbrush, these cliffs were invisible until it was too late. Many a tale recounted in the village spoke of wanderers, entranced by the spirit's glow, stepping off into the abyss, their last moments marked by a chilling realization of the deceitful light.

However, Callum was an avid explorer with decades of experience under his belt. He was well versed in the language of the wilderness and skilled in reading the subtle signs of nature, from the direction of the wind to the patterns of the stars. In his heart, Callum believed that only fools could fall prey to the tricks of the will-o'-the-wisp. As an expert woodsman, he was confident in his ability to navigate any terrain, no matter how treacherous or unfamiliar.

With this unshakable confidence, Callum's curiosity about the will-o'-the-wisp grew ever stronger. He thought of it not as a threat but as a challenge, a test of his skills and experience. He was sure that he could outwit the spirit and uncover the secrets it guarded in the deep wilderness. To him, the tales of the will-o'-the-wisp leading people to their doom were nothing but stories for the gullible and the unskilled.

One moonlit night, Callum set out into the forest, determined to track down the elusive spirit. He moved with ease, his steps silent and sure, his eyes keenly observing every detail around him. As he ventured deeper, the familiar sights and sounds of the forest comforted him, reinforcing his belief in his mastery over the wild.

Callum's determination eventually bore fruit. He spotted the mysterious light of the will-o'-the-wisp twinkling between the trees. It moved with an elegant grace, always just out of reach yet never completely vanishing. Excited, Callum followed the light. He moved carefully but confidently, certain of his ability to retrace his steps.

The light led him on a winding path through the forest. He crossed over babbling streams and pushed through dense thickets. Callum's senses were heightened, keenly picking up any subtle changes around him. He noted landmarks, mentally mapping his route.

But as the night wore on, the forest seemed to transform. The trees appeared less familiar, the sounds more eerie, and the air grew thick with a mist that obscured the moon. Callum realized, with a rising sense of unease, that the landscape had changed subtly, almost imperceptibly, disorienting even his experienced eyes.

The light of the will-o'-the-wisp, which had initially drawn Callum in with its mystery, now appeared to taunt him with its elusive movements. Callum pushed on, refusing to admit that he might have underestimated the spirit. Suddenly, he found himself on the edge of a steep ravine, hidden by the dense fog and the deceptive light. It was at this moment that Callum realized the true nature of the will-o'-the-wisp. It was not just a physical guide leading travelers astray; it was also a master of illusion, capable of altering perceptions and challenging even the most experienced woodsman.

With a newfound respect for the legend and its dangers, Callum carefully retraced his steps, using all his skills to navigate back to familiar ground. He emerged from the forest as dawn broke, humbled and wiser. His encounter with the will-o'-the-wisp had taught him that even the most skilled are not immune to the powers of the Otherworld.

Back in the village, Callum shared his tale, not as a story of triumph but as a lesson in humility and respect for the ancient mysteries of the land. The will-o'-the-wisp remained a legend, a symbol of the wild, untamed spirit of the Scottish wilderness, and a reminder that some mysteries are best left unchallenged.

Chapter 5: Ghosts and Apparitions

Edinburgh, nestled in the heart of Scotland, is a city where the modern world intertwines with the past. Today, it bursts with a mix of contemporary culture and historical magnificence, but beneath its modern facade lies a deep and sometimes dark history.

In medieval Scotland, Edinburgh was more than just a city; it was the heart of a nation. The castles, including the renowned Edinburgh Castle, were not just residences but also symbols of power and protection. Built on a rock, the castle overlooked the city, a guardian against invaders and a stronghold for the rulers of Scotland. These castles were the epicenters of political power and military might. They were designed to withstand sieges and protect their inhabitants from the tumultuous world outside.

Edinburgh Castle.

Kim Traynor, CC BY-SA 3.0 <https://creativecommons.org/licenses/by-sa/3.0>, via Wikimedia Commons: https://commons.wikimedia.org/wiki/File:Edinburgh_Castle_from_the_North.JPG

Yet, amidst the tangible history of battles and kings, a different kind of legacy lingers in Edinburgh's cobbled streets and ancient buildings—a legacy of secrets, myths, and eerie tales.

Among these secrets was a network of hidden tunnels beneath Edinburgh Castle. They were believed to have been constructed for covert purposes, perhaps as secret escape routes for royalty or as a means to move unseen during times of war or political turmoil. While their true purpose remains shrouded in mystery, the rediscovery of these secret tunnels eventually led to the beginning of a haunting story popularly known as the Ghost Piper of Edinburgh Castle.

The legend goes that immediately after the discovery of the tunnels, the city's leaders announced that they needed someone to explore the labyrinthine network. They wanted to unravel the mystery of these subterranean passageways. Thus, for unknown reasons, a young piper was chosen to carry out this task. In the boy's eyes, his mission was simple: he was to navigate the network of tunnels while playing his pipes so that those above could trace his progress through the melodies echoing from below.

The young piper delved into the darkness. The tune coming from his bagpipes resonated through the streets, creating an otherworldly atmosphere that captivated the city. People paused in their daily chores, listening intently as the haunting notes floated up from the depths. Some followed the sound, tracking his path through the city, while others were tasked with creating a map of the tunnels based on the rough location of the boy deep underneath the cobblestone streets.

But then, something chilling occurred. In the midst of his exploration, the music stopped abruptly. The silence that followed was deafening, a stark contrast to the lively tunes that had filled the air moments before. The last notes were heard near Tron Kirk. Reports were presumably made to the city's leaders. Almost immediately, a frantic search was mounted, but no trace of the young piper was ever found. He had vanished, mysteriously swallowed by the labyrinth beneath the city. In the wake of his mysterious disappearance, the tunnels were sealed as if to bury the secret of what happened to the young piper. However, the story does not end there.

Today, it is said that the eerie sound of bagpipes can still be heard beneath the streets of Edinburgh, especially near the castle. The music is a haunting reminder of the boy who never returned, his spirit seemingly trapped in the labyrinth, playing his pipes in a perpetual search for a way out. Perhaps he is waiting for someone to rescue him from his eternal entrapment.

These ghostly melodies are not constant. They occur at unexpected moments, sending shivers down the spines of those who hear them. The whispers of the past seem louder in the quiet of the night. Some say it is nothing but the wind, while others believe it is the young piper's ghost, still wandering the tunnels, lost and alone.

The Ghost Piper of Edinburgh Castle is just one of many ghostly tales from Scotland's past. Another haunting narrative resides in the shadowy halls of Crathes Castle.

Built in the 16th century by Alexander Burnett, the castle rose from the Royal Forest of Drum. This classic Scottish tower-house-style castle, with its imposing structure, began its construction in 1553. However, its completion was delayed, largely due to the political unrest involving Mary, Queen of Scots. The castle was finally finished in 1596.

The story of Crathes Castle is intertwined with the dark and tragic tale of the Burnetts of Leys. Before the castle's construction, the Burnetts resided in a house near a loch, a place that became the scene of a chilling event. This event, marked by death and spectral hauntings, would forever alter the destiny of the Burnett family.

It began with Alexander Burnett, a young lord who came under the strict supervision of his controlling mother, Lady Agnes, following his father's passing. Alexander's life took a fateful turn when he fell in love with Bertha, a distant cousin who had been entrusted to his family's care. However, their blossoming love was to be short-lived. Alexander, having been away, returned to find Bertha on her deathbed.

In a moment of profound grief, Alexander reached for a goblet of wine, perhaps to share a final drink with his beloved, but Lady Agnes intervened. With a swift motion, she snatched the goblet from his hand and hurled it out the window. It was then that a horrifying truth dawned on Alexander: his mother had poisoned Bertha. Lady Agnes had always displayed her disapproval whenever Alexander expressed his fondness for Bertha. She was said to have another plan for his son; she wished for him to marry into a noble family instead.

The tragedy at the Loch house took a more sinister turn months later. Bertha's father arrived, intending to bring his daughter home, only to be confronted with the grim news of her death. As Lady Agnes attempted to explain the circumstances, a bone-chilling cold swept through the room.

Suddenly, Lady Agnes, her eyes wide with terror, screamed, "She comes! She comes!" and suddenly fell dead to the floor, frozen.

Plagued by the haunting events and the specter of death, the Burnetts abandoned their old Loch house and sought refuge in Crathes Castle, hoping to leave behind the ghosts of their past. However, the spirits would not be so easily forgotten. On the anniversary of Bertha's death, a phantom spirit known as the White Lady is said to make the journey from the old Loch house to Crathes Castle. Some believe this ghostly figure to be Bertha, stuck forever seeking justice and peace. Others whisper that it is none other than Lady Agnes, cursed to relive her treachery for eternity.

Crathes Castle.

Crathes Castle is home to multiple ghost stories. There's also the haunting account of the Green Lady.

The Green Lady is often spotted silently gliding through the rooms and hallways of Crathes Castle. She is believed to be a former inhabitant of the castle, but her identity has been lost to the ages. She is most often seen in a specific room, now named the Green Lady's Room. Her appearances are always accompanied by a sudden drop in temperature and a subtle scent of rosemary, a herb traditionally associated with remembrance.

Legend has it that the Green Lady was a servant girl at Crathes Castle who fell victim to a tragic fate. The most common telling of her story suggests a tale of forbidden love and heartbreak. She was believed to have fallen in love with a nobleman residing at the castle, a love that was doomed from the start due to their different social standings. Their secret romance ended in tragedy when the girl found herself with child.

Faced with the harsh realities of her situation and the unforgiving societal norms of the time, the Green Lady's fate took a dark turn. It is said that she vanished mysteriously, with whispers suggesting that she might have been killed to prevent a scandal or perhaps took her own life.

Many years after the Green Lady's mysterious vanishing, something unsettling was found during renovations at the castle. Workers uncovered the skeletal remains of a woman and a child concealed behind a fireplace in the Green Lady's Room. This grim find gave a hauntingly real aspect to the ghost stories, hinting that the Green Lady's unsettled spirit could be roaming the castle, grieving her lost love and the child she never had the chance to raise.

To this day, the Green Lady's spirit lingers in the Crathes Castle. Visitors and staff members often report seeing her spectral form. Some even say they feel a deep sense of sorrow in the room where she was last seen, the room now named after her. Others describe an eerie sensation of being watched or catching glimpses of a figure in green out of the corner of their eye, only for it to vanish as soon as they turn to look directly at it. A few also claim that they heard distant voices warning them not to enter the room, causing them to hesitate and turn back.

Hermitage Castle

Hermitage Castle, nestled in the rugged borderlands of Scotland, holds stories of intrigue, betrayal, and ghostly whispers within its imposing walls. This formidable fortress, often referred to as "the guardhouse of the bloodiest valley in Britain," has stood since the 12th century.

Hermitage Castle in 1814.
https://commons.wikimedia.org/wiki/File:Hermitagecastle1814.jpg

One of the most notable episodes in the castle's history involves Sir William Douglas, known as "the Knight of Liddesdale." In 1338, during the Wars of Scottish Independence, Douglas wrestled Hermitage Castle from the clutches of its English occupant, Sir Ralph Neville. The seizure of Hermitage was a strategic victory, with Douglas employing a combination of military prowess and cunning tactics. His success in these conflicts earned him a formidable reputation and significant respect in Scotland, marking him as a key figure in the struggle against English domination.

However, Sir William's story becomes more complex and darker with the appearance of Sir Alexander Ramsay. Ramsay, another distinguished Scottish knight, rose to prominence and was appointed as the sheriff of Teviotdale, a position that Douglas long had his eyes on. Ramsay's growing influence and success, particularly his capture of Roxburgh Castle from the English, only fueled Douglas's envy and resentment.

Driven by jealousy, Sir William Douglas conceived a sinister plan. He lured Sir Alexander Ramsay to Hermitage Castle under the guise of friendship or for a meeting. However, upon Ramsay's arrival, Douglas's true intentions were revealed. Ramsay was seized and thrown into a deep, dark dungeon within the castle's bowels. This "frightful pit," as it came to be known, was a place of unimaginable horrors. Devoid of light, air, and even basic sanitation, it was more like a living tomb. It was far worse than the cells that held the most notorious criminals or the dens that housed the world's wildest animals.

In this ghastly dungeon, Sir Alexander Ramsay suffered a fate worse than death. He was left to starve with no hope of rescue. The conditions were so dire that it was said he resorted to eating pieces of his own flesh before he finally succumbed to death's embrace. Ramsay's tragic demise was more than just a tale of brutal revenge; it's a stark illustration of the unforgiving and relentless quest for power among medieval Scottish nobility.

The ghostly legacy of this dark deed has haunted Hermitage Castle ever since. It is said that the anguished groans of Sir Alexander Ramsay echo through the castle. Visitors to Hermitage have reported hearing unsettling sounds emanating from the depths of the castle, almost as if the very stones themselves are reliving the horrors of the past.

However, not all ghostly tales surrounding Hermitage Castle are terrifying and eerie. Among the castle's storied past is a tale of love and dedication involving one of Scotland's most famous historical figures, Mary, Queen of Scots.

The story takes us back to the 16ᵗʰ century, during the tumultuous period of Mary's reign. One of the central figures in her life was James Hepburn, 4ᵗʰ Earl of Bothwell, a man who would eventually become Mary's third husband. Bothwell, a loyal supporter of Mary, was often involved in the political and military unrest of the time.

On one fateful occasion, Lord Bothwell found himself gravely wounded following a skirmish with border reivers, who were an infamous band of raiders in the area between Scotland and England. The news of his injury reached Mary, Queen of Scots, who was staying in Jedburgh at the time, approximately fifty miles away from Hermitage Castle, where Bothwell was recovering.

Upon hearing of Bothwell's condition, Mary made a daring decision. She resolved to visit Bothwell. It was a journey fraught with danger, not only because of the distance but also due to the chaotic political climate and the rough terrain she would have to traverse. Undeterred, Mary set out on her journey, riding through the rugged landscape of the Scottish Borders. Her ride to Hermitage Castle became legendary for its speed and her determination. Mary covered the fifty-mile distance in just a single day, an impressive achievement given the travel difficulties of the period.

Upon her arrival at Hermitage Castle, Mary found Bothwell in a dire state, though, fortunately, he survived. Mary's return journey proved to be even more harrowing. The journey, coupled with the stress and strain of the situation, took a significant toll on her health.

Upon her return to Jedburgh, Mary fell gravely ill. She developed a fever so severe that it nearly claimed her life. Her visit to Hermitage, though brief, was a poignant moment, reflecting the depth of her concern for her future husband. This act of bravery and devotion adds a bright light to the otherwise grim history of Hermitage Castle. Today, some claim they caught a glimpse of the apparitions of Mary and Bothwell walking around the castle, their hands tightly wrapped around each other.

Mary King's Close

In the center of Edinburgh, along the famous Royal Mile, stands the Edinburgh City Chambers, a prominent and stately building. This impressive structure holds a secret buried beneath its foundations: a hidden network of streets and homes known as Mary's Close.

This close, which was built in the 17th century, was named after Mary King, a well-known merchant of the time. Her name became forever linked to this hidden corner of the city, marking a place that once buzzed with life but now echoes with the tales of its haunting past.

Mary King's Close, Edinburgh.
https://commons.wikimedia.org/wiki/File:Marykingsclose006.jpg

Imagine seeing this close through the eyes of a young man named John, who lived there in the 17th century. For him and his neighbors, life in Mary's Close was a daily struggle. The streets were narrow and dark, with houses piled upon each other (sometimes rising up to seven stories). Those with more wealth were said to have lived on the top floors, while the less unfortunate ones inhabited the lower stories. To put it simply, Mary's Close was a cramped labyrinth of shadowy passageways. While the place was teeming with life, the air was also filled with the filth and stench of an era devoid of modern sanitation.

In John's time, Mary's Close was marred by the absence of a proper sewage system. Residents, John included, had to deal with the daily challenge of getting rid of their own waste. Each household was equipped bucket, which was their only means of managing waste. When the ,et was full, they would wait for a shout of "Gardy Loo!" from the streets. This shout marked that it was time to throw the waste out onto the street. The waste would flow down the streets in little channels, eventually ending up in a big, dirty manmade lake called Nor' Loch, where the Princes Street Gardens are now.

This lack of sanitation definitely made Mary's Close a breeding ground for disease, and it was also here that the Black Death found fertile ground in 1645. The plague tore through the cramped quarters with ruthless efficiency, leaving nothing but a trail of death and despair. In a desperate, misguided attempt to halt the spread of the contagion, the city's authorities made a harrowing decision. They sealed off the neighborhood, trapping the residents within the plague-ridden close.

John, along with his neighbors, faced a grim fate as the walls went up. Left to die in conditions of unimaginable horror, Mary's Close became a tomb for its inhabitants. Once the plague had subsided, the task of removing the dead was as gruesome as it was necessary. Butchers were sent in to carry out the dreadful work, dismembering the decomposing bodies and carting them away.

Since then, people have said that Mary's Close transformed into a realm of ghosts, as the spirits of those who perished under such tragic circumstances were not easily put to rest. The story of Thomas Coltheart, a lawyer who lived there later, is one of the most famous. He and his wife saw strange things in their home. They saw the head of an old man with a long beard and scary eyes floating around. Sometimes, a hand appeared, trying to shake Thomas's hand. The sight of a ghostly child hovering in mid-air was pretty common, while deformed phantom animals added to the surreal spectacle.

Yet, it was the spirit of a little girl, discovered by a Japanese medium, that left a profound impact on people. The medium, overwhelmed by a heavy, depressive aura, encountered the ghost of a young girl who had died from the plague. She mourned not only her life but also her lost doll. In response to her sorrow, the television crew and subsequent visitors began leaving gifts for her. Now, a collection of toys, dolls, books, and coins lies in the corner of the room, serving as a tribute to the girl's lost innocence and the tragic history of Mary's Close.

The popular belief that Mary's Close was sealed with plague victims inside in 1645 is a tale that has captivated many. However, there's another side to the story, a view that contradicts this grim narrative and sheds a different light on the history of the close.

Contrary to the belief that the close was a sealed tomb for its plague-ridden residents, historical records suggest that those healthy enough or willing to move were relocated to Burgh Muir, an area outside the city. For those who chose to stay, life in Mary's Close went on, albeit under the dark shadow of the plague. These residents continued their daily routines and even ran their businesses amidst the crisis. Houses affected by the plague were marked with white flags, signaling the need for food and coal. This system allowed council workers and volunteers to provide necessary supplies to those in quarantine.

One figure who played a crucial role during this time was George Rae, a plague doctor known for his visits to Mary's Close. Rae, like other plague doctors of his time, wore a striking and somewhat bizarre outfit. He wore a mask shaped like a crow's beak and was dressed head to toe in leather. The mask was not just for show. The beak was stuffed with herbs and flowers with strong scents, which were thought to keep away the airborne diseases that were believed to spread the plague. In reality, the disease was spread by bacteria, and Rae's leather outfit inadvertently protected him from the bites of fleas that carried the plague.

The mask of a plague doctor.

Rae's methods for treating the plague were as extreme as his appearance. He would cut open the boils of plague victims to drain the pus, then seal the wounds with a red-hot poker. While this technique sounds horrific, it surprisingly saved many lives.

Because of the dangers involved, plague doctors like Rae were promised financial rewards by the city council for their risky, life-saving work. However, when it came time to pay, the council broke their promise, leaving many doctors, including Rae, uncompensated for their efforts. It's believed that Rae never received full payment for his heroic actions and lived out his days without due recognition.

Despite the efforts of Rae and others, many residents of Mary's Close succumbed to the plague. Yet, the close was never sealed off as is often believed. Its history took another turn in the 18th century with the construction of the Royal Exchange. This development led to the demolition and burial of part of the close. It remained accessible, with a few small businesses operating within, including the Cheney family's saw business, which lasted until 1902.

After the Cheney family left, Mary's Close was finally sealed off and forgotten, only to be rediscovered years later during a roadworks project when workers accidentally broke through into the hidden close. During World War II, the close served as a bomb shelter, lying dormant again until the 1990s. It was then that Mary King's Close was reopened as the fascinating tourist attraction we see today, a place that continues to intrigue and haunt visitors with its complex and layered history.

Chapter 6: The Mysterious Creatures of Scottish Folklore

The story begins on a misty evening in a small village nestled not far from the shores of a tranquil loch. There, we find a sad little boy. He had just stormed out of his house following a heated dispute with his mother over his wish to stay at his friend's house for the night. Frustrated and thinking that his mother would never understand him, the little boy decided to calm himself by walking to his favorite spot by the loch.

As soon as he arrived, the boy sat on the boulder by the loch, enjoying the peace that nature offered. Nearly half an hour passed, and he noticed that the sky had begun to turn dark. As he stood up, preparing to make his way home, the little boy saw something he had never seen before in his life.

The surface of the loch stirred, and from the depths emerged a majestic horse. Its coat shimmered like the midnight sea, and its eyes gleamed with an otherworldly light. To the little boy, the mysterious horse appeared not as a beast to fear but as a beautiful creature, inviting him for a ride. The water horse, known as the each-uisge, let out a nicker that echoed like a distant melody, enticing the little boy to come closer. The boy, though wary, felt a strange pull, a curiosity that overrode the cautionary tales he had grown up with. In a moment of boldness or perhaps folly, the innocent little boy reached out and touched the creature, its coat cool and smooth under his fingers.

Sensing no danger, the boy mounted the beast, his face full of excitement, as he had never ridden such a magnificent mount before. But the creature had its own intention. A second later, the each-uisge revealed itself. Its eyes suddenly turned dark as the abyss, and its smooth body began to change, growing slick and wet. Startled by the transformation, the little boy tried to dismount the beast, but both of his hands were stuck to the water horse's wet coat. The boy desperately screamed for help, drawing the attention of a passerby who was returning from the next village, but it was too late.

The each-uisge, with a strength that belied its graceful form, quickly plunged into the depths, dragging the helpless boy with it. The loch churned and roiled as the water horse descended, revealing its true nature as a predator of the deep. The passerby, having witnessed the incident, could do nothing but stand by the shore, his face stricken with horror and trauma as the boy's screams faded into the night.

Legend has it that the each-uisge devoured its victims, leaving nothing but the liver to float to the surface. As the passerby waited with bated breath, a grim sign emerged from the loch: a liver, the last remnant of the poor boy.

From that day forth, the tale of the boy and the each-uisge became a cautionary story passed down through generations. Parents warned their children of the dangers lurking in the depths of the lochs and of the water horse that could charm and deceive, its beauty masking a deadly nature.

The supposed skeleton of an each-uisge displayed in the garden of a house in Ord.
John Allan / Each Uisge Earballach:

Yet, the lochs weren't the only places where caution was advised. The Scots were equally warned of the dangers lurking in streams and rivers; these were the domains of the kelpies. These mystical creatures were capable of transforming from their equine form into human figures, and they have been the subject of many tales. A peculiar characteristic often gave away their true identity: the presence of water weeds in their hair, a subtle hint of their aquatic origins.

One such tale, recounted by the Scottish folklorist Walter Gregor, tells of a kelpie that assumed the form of a wizened old man. This figure was often seen muttering to himself while sitting on a bridge, deeply focused on stitching a pair of trousers. His presence, which was eerie and out of place, aroused suspicion among the locals. One day, a passerby, convinced that the old man was a kelpie in disguise, struck him on the head. The blow caused the kelpie to revert to its true form, and it quickly scampered away to the safety of its lair in a nearby pond.

Other accounts of kelpies in human form are more sinister. Some describe a rough, shaggy man who would leap behind a lone traveler, gripping and crushing him. Others speak of kelpies tearing apart and devouring their human victims.

A particular folktale from Barra, an island off the coast of Scotland, offers a different perspective on the nature of kelpies. This story revolves around a lonely kelpie that transformed itself into a handsome young man, hoping to woo a young girl and make her his wife. However, the sharp and observant girl recognized the young man for what he truly was. While he slept, she removed his silver necklace, which was actually his bridle, causing him to revert back to his horse form.

The Kelpies, thirty-meter-high sculptures in Grangemouth depicting the mythical creatures.

Instead of fearing the kelpie, the girl saw an opportunity. She took the transformed kelpie back to her father's farm, where she put it to work for a full year. At the year's end, she rode the kelpie to consult a wise man. Following the wise man's advice, she returned the silver necklace to the kelpie, which allowed him to regain his human form.

The wise man then posed a question to the kelpie: would he choose to remain a kelpie or become a mortal man? The kelpie, in turn, asked the girl if she would agree to be his wife were he a man. When she confirmed she would, the kelpie, without hesitation, made the choice to become mortal. The story ends with their marriage, a union that transformed the once-lonely and potentially malevolent kelpie into a loving husband, illustrating the transformative power of love and understanding.

This tale of the kelpie diverges from the more common narratives of an evil creature, offering a glimpse into the complexity of these mythical creatures. It suggests that beneath their fearsome exterior, there may be a longing for connection, understanding, and perhaps redemption, themes that resonate deeply in the rich folklore of Scotland.

The Legendary Loch Ness Monster

Loch Ness is an expansive body of water, stretching over 22 square miles and plunging to depths of over 750 feet. It is not just one of Scotland's largest lochs by volume but also a treasure trove of ancient myths and legends. Its most famous inhabitant, the Loch Ness Monster, affectionately known as Nessie, has captured the world's imagination.

Loch Ness, Scotland's largest loch by volume.
Sam Fentress, CC BY-SA 2.0 <https://creativecommons.org/licenses/by-sa/2.0>, via Wikimedia Commons: https://commons.wikimedia.org/wiki/File:LochNessUrquhart.jpg

The legend of Nessie dates back to ancient times, with the first recorded sighting attributed to the revered Irish missionary Saint Columba in 565 CE.

As the story goes, Saint Columba was traveling through the Scottish Highlands, spreading the Christian faith among the Pictish tribes. His journey brought him to the shores of Loch Ness.

One day, as Columba and his companions were near the loch, they came upon a group of locals burying a man by the water's edge. They inquired about what had happened and were shocked by the tragic tale. The man had been swimming in the loch when he was suddenly attacked and killed by a monstrous creature that lurked in its depths. The locals spoke of the beast with a mix of fear and awe, describing it as a creature unlike any other, a terror of the deep that had claimed the lives of many.

Undeterred by the grim stories, Saint Columba was determined to cross the loch. He instructed one of his followers, a man named Lugne Mocumin, to swim across the water and bring back a boat from the other side. As Lugne obediently plunged into the dark, cold waters, a sense of dread fell over the onlookers, for they knew the beast lay hidden below.

True to their fears, as Lugne swam, the waters of the loch began to churn. From the depths emerged the monstrous creature, its great head and long neck surging toward the defenseless swimmer. The onlookers cried out in terror, certain that Lugne would meet the same fate as the man they had just buried. But Saint Columba stood firm on the shore, showing no sign of fear. Instead, he raised his hand and, with a powerful voice, invoked the name of God, commanding the beast, "Go no further. Do not touch the man. Go back at once." To the amazement of all, the creature halted as if struck by an invisible force. It then turned and disappeared back into the depths of the loch, leaving Lugne unharmed.

Unless one is a true believer of Nessie, it is easy to see this as a tale made up to symbolize the power of faith and the triumph of good over the unseen evils of the world. Over the centuries, the legend of Nessie grew, with the mysterious depths of Loch Ness providing the perfect backdrop for the creature's elusive nature. The ancient Picts, known for their intricate stone carvings, depicted a mysterious beast with flippers, suggesting that belief in such a creature has been a part of local culture for millennia.

Swedish naturalist Bengt Sjogren proposed that Nessie's legend might be linked to kelpie myths, suggesting a shared origin in Scottish folklore.

However, others believe Nessie is a separate being altogether. Unlike the shape-shifting kelpies, Nessie is often described as a giant sea serpent, stirring the waters of Loch Ness with its movements.

Eyewitness accounts of Nessie vary, but a common description is that of a massive creature with two or three humps protruding above the water's surface. However, these sightings have been met with much skepticism. Experts suggest that such observations could be optical illusions, possibly caused by boat wakes on the loch's surface or even by birds or other wildlife.

The most widely accepted depiction of Nessie is that of a plesiosaur, a prehistoric marine reptile. This image was popularized by several notable sightings and photographs. In 1934, Arthur Grant, a veterinary student, claimed to have a close encounter with the creature, describing it as having a long neck and a small head. This account was soon followed by the infamous "Surgeon's Photograph," which appears to show Nessie with a long neck and small head, like a plesiosaur.

The Loch Ness Monster, As Sketched by Mr. A. Grant From Lieut.-Commander Gould's Interesting Monograph Upon the Subject.

A drawing of Nessie by Arthur Grant.
https://commons.wikimedia.org/wiki/File:Arthur_Grant_loch_ness_sketch.png

However, this theory presents several issues. Loch Ness was formed after the last ice age, so it would have been uninhabitable by a prehistoric reptile like the plesiosaur. Furthermore, as a reptile, such a creature would need to surface frequently for air, leading to the expectation of more frequent sightings than have been reported.

Despite these challenges, the legend of Nessie continues to be a symbol of mystery and fascination. The story of the Loch Ness Monster transcends the realm of folklore and has become a cultural phenomenon. It draws thousands of visitors to Loch Ness each year, with people hoping to catch a glimpse of the elusive creature.

The allure of Nessie lies not just in the mystery of its existence but also in the human fascination with the unknown. The Loch Ness Monster embodies the unexplained and the undiscovered, fueling our imagination and inviting endless speculation and debate.

So, it is no surprise that the legend of Nessie has evolved over the years, with numerous hoaxes and scientific expeditions adding layers to the story. From sonar scans to underwater photography, efforts to prove or disprove Nessie's existence have only heightened the intrigue. Each unexplained sighting or blurry photograph adds to the lore, keeping the legend alive in the hearts and minds of believers and skeptics alike.

Redcaps

Redcaps, also known as powries or dunters, are said to be small, stout, and incredibly strong creatures. They dwell in the ruined castles and towers along the Scottish Borders. These beings, as described by 19th-century folklorist William Henderson, are among the most sinister in Scottish folklore.

Redcaps are, of course, characterized by their red caps. These caps are central to their very existence. The caps are dyed in human blood, which the redcaps are compelled to replenish by committing murder. Should the blood in the cap dry up, it is believed that the redcap would die.

These creatures are often depicted as old, wiry men with long, sharp talons and teeth. Their eyes gleam with a malevolent light, and they wear iron boots that clank ominously as they move. Redcaps are swift and merciless. They are known for their brutality and for haunting the sites of tyranny and bloodshed.

One of the most famous tales of the murderous redcaps took place in a dark, dilapidated castle in the Scottish Borders. This castle, once a site of great battles, had become the perfect abode for a redcap. In the tale, a wandering traveler seeking shelter for the night stumbled upon the castle. Unaware of its sinister inhabitant, he entered, looking for a place to rest. As night fell, the castle's eerie silence was broken by the sound of heavy, iron-clad footsteps. The traveler, filled with dread, quickly rose to his feet and hid in the shadows, watching in horror as the redcap appeared.

The creature was indeed grotesque, with twisted features and a cap soaked in fresh blood. Its eyes glowed as it scoured the castle for its next victim. The traveler, realizing the grave danger he was in, knew he must escape before he was spotted.

As the redcap approached his hiding place, the traveler remembered a piece of lore he had heard in his travels: redcaps could be repelled by words of scripture or by the cross. With no cross in hand, he recited verses from the Bible he had learned in his youth. As he spoke the sacred words, the redcap let out a furious howl and recoiled as if struck by an unseen force. Seizing the opportunity, the traveler fled the castle without ever looking back despite the sounds of the redcap's enraged screams echoing behind him. He ran through the night, not stopping until the castle was far behind him.

The most well-known story is about Robin Redcap, the most notorious redcap, and his connection with Lord William de Soulis. Lord William, a 13th-century nobleman, was infamous for his brutal rule and involvement in black magic. He was widely feared and despised throughout the Scottish Borders for his extreme cruelty. He lived in the ominous Hermitage Castle, which we talked about in a previous chapter.

According to legend, Lord Soulis was not alone in his nefarious activities. He had a companion by his side, a redcap named Robin. Unlike the common redcaps known for haunting dilapidated castles, Robin Redcap was bound to Lord Soulis, serving as his familiar and aiding in his dark rituals. His cap was often drenched in the blood of his lord's victims, and he was said to possess strength far greater than his size would suggest.

The locals believed that Lord Soulis and Robin Redcap engaged in abominable acts, including the abduction and sacrifice of children. The pair's reign of terror reached a peak with a dark scheme in which Lord Soulis, with Robin Redcap's help, sought to bind the dark forces to his will.

The local populace decided to put an end to Lord Soulis's tyranny. Legend has it that the local wise men, knowing that neither steel nor rope could kill a warlock, captured Lord Soulis and boiled him alive in a cauldron at Ninestane Rig. As for Robin Redcap, his evil spirit was said to have vanished into thin air after the death of his master.

The ghost of Sir William de Soulis is said to still haunt the corridors of Hermitage Castle. Visitors to the castle have reported eerie occurrences, with some claiming to hear the heart-rending sobs of children echoing through the crumbling corridors.

It is said that Robin's malevolent spirit also still lingers in the ruins of Hermitage Castle. Visitors to the castle have reported feeling an ominous presence, and some claim to have seen a small, wizened figure with a blood-red cap quietly watching them from the shadows.

Selkies

In the pantheon of Scottish mythological creatures, the selkies hold a unique place. Unlike the brutal kelpies or the sinister redcaps, selkies are known for their kind and benevolent nature. They are said to have aided children and fishermen lost at sea.

These gentle creatures of the sea are known for their ability to transform and for their mesmerizing singing voices. Their songs, often heard along the shores and cliffs of the Orkney and Shetland Islands, are said to be so captivating that they can soothe the restless sea and enchant anyone who hears them.

In Scottish lore, the selkie's ability to shift between seal and human form is closely connected to their seal skin. A selkie must carefully guard their precious skin; without it, they are unable to return to their original form. If a selkie's skin is lost or stolen, they will be bound to the land and unable to return to the sea. When selkies are in their human form, they are famous for their extraordinary beauty and elegance, often captivating the hearts of those who encounter them.

A depiction of selkies on a stamp originating from the Faroe Islands.
https://commons.wikimedia.org/wiki/File:Faroese_stamp_579_the_seal_woman.jpg

The most well-known tale about the selkies is the touching story of "The Selkie Bride." This tale begins with a lonely fisherman who lived by the sea. He spent his days watching the seals along the shore, but he was particularly drawn to one beautiful selkie who would shed her skin and bask in the sun.

One evening, driven by a desire for companionship, the fisherman stealthily approached the selkie while she was in human form and stole her seal skin. Without it, she could not return to the sea. The fisherman, overcome with love and longing, begged her to stay and be his wife. And so, the selkie, unable to return to her home without her skin, reluctantly agreed.

They lived together for many years, and the selkie bride bore the fisherman several children. Although she was a loving wife and mother, a part of her always yearned for the sea. Her heart ached for her true home, and she would often gaze longingly at the ocean for hours, dreaming and reminiscing about her life beneath the waves.

One day, one of her children discovered a seal skin in their home. Not realizing its significance, the child brought it to her mother. Overwhelmed with both joy and sadness, the selkie knew she had to make a difficult choice. That evening, as the sun dipped below the horizon, she kissed her children goodbye, donned her seal skin, and returned to the sea.

The fisherman eventually returned to find his wife gone. He searched the shore in vain, calling her name repeatedly, but she was nowhere to be found. From that day forward, he would often see a seal watching him from the waves, its eyes reflecting a deep understanding and love. The fisherman knew it was his beloved selkie bride, watching over him and their children from her home in the sea.

While many stories of selkies feature female beings, male selkies also occupy a significant place in Scottish folklore. Male selkies are often portrayed as irresistible to mortal women, especially those who are unhappy or longing for their husbands who have gone to sea. Legends say that male selkies are particularly drawn to married women who yearn for something beyond their mundane lives.

According to legend, if a woman wishes to summon a male selkie, she must weep seven tears into the sea. This act of sorrow and longing is said to call forth a selkie man from the depths of the ocean. He will then offer the love and companionship she truly desires.

The lore surrounding selkies is rich and varied. Some stories suggest that selkies can only shed their skins and take on human form once every seven years. This limitation adds a sense of fleeting magic and rarity to their interactions with humans. Other tales hint at a more mystical origin for the selkies. Some believe that selkies were once humans who committed sinful acts and were transformed as a punishment. Others view them as fallen angels, creatures of divine beauty and grace that do not quite belong to either the world of humans or the realm of the divine.

Despite all these different interpretations of selkie tales, the themes of transformation and longing are always present. Selkies, whether seen as magical creatures or as humans cursed to live in two worlds, represent the timeless desire for connection, freedom, and the exploration of one's true nature.

Chapter 7: Witchcraft, Dark Magic, and Curses

Centuries ago, in a small village on the east of Scotland, lived a man who had been plagued by a series of unfortunate events. He had lost his mother the previous winter, followed by his only son the next spring. To make matters worse, his crops failed, and his livestock grew sickly. It appeared as though the misfortunes followed him day and night, casting a dark shadow over his life.

As the days turned into months, the man's melancholy only deepened. He watched as his once-prosperous life crumbled around him. But there was one constant presence in his life, the woman who had stood by his side through thick and thin—his wife. She had been a source of comfort and solace in his darkest hours.

However, grief can be a poison that distorts one's thoughts and perceptions. The man's grief began to turn into suspicion, and he grew increasingly paranoid. He noticed that his wife would occasionally slip out of their quiet cottage at night, leaving him alone in the darkness. His mind raced with thoughts of betrayal and deceit, and he started to believe that his wife was involved in dark deeds.

One day, he confided in his neighbors, voicing his suspicions to them in hushed tones. They, too, had noticed his wife's nighttime wanderings and began to share his apprehension. Rumors spread like wildfire through the village, and before long, everyone believed that the man's wife was a witch, practicing dark magic under the secret of night.

The man's accusations became louder and more insistent. He proclaimed to anyone who would listen that his wife was a witch, capable of cursing the land and causing misfortune. By this time, it was clear that his grief had driven him to madness, and he couldn't see the truth. His wife was merely seeking solace in the stillness of the night to try to ease her own worries and sadness.

The villagers, swayed by the man's relentless accusations, gathered on one fateful evening and confronted the accused woman. She pleaded her innocence, tears streaming down her cheeks, her voice breaking, but her protests fell on deaf ears. Fear and hysteria had taken hold of the villagers, and they wanted to rid their community of the supposed witch.

In a chaotic and somber ceremony, the woman was banished from the village, the only home she had ever known. The woman looked at his husband, hoping he would come to her defense, yet his eyes showed no remorse. It was as if he was disgusted by her very presence. And so, she left, heartbroken and alone, disappearing into the dense woods with nowhere else to go and no one to turn to. What happened to her afterward remained a mystery. Some claimed she eventually managed to rebuild her life far from the village that condemned her, but she no longer knew how to smile or laugh. Others suggested that she met her demise in the woods, perhaps killed by wild beasts that roamed the area.

In the folklore of the Scottish people, magic was seen as a mix of both good and evil. They believed in kind fairies and spirits that could bring luck and happiness, but they also harbored a strong fear of witchcraft and its potential for harm.

In the Middle Ages, when superstitions ran rampant, women were often the targets of accusations of witchcraft. This was partly due to societal norms, as women were seen as having a closer connection to the mystical and the unknown compared to men. Their roles as healers and midwives made them susceptible to suspicion, and their knowledge of herbs and remedies sometimes fueled accusations of witchcraft.

Witchcraft in Scotland was characterized by the use of black magic to bring harm to others. Witches were believed to have obtained their powers either through initiation into a coven or through inheritance. They were seen as agents of the devil, practitioners of evil, and purveyors of malevolent spells.

One of the most chilling aspects of witchcraft was the belief that witches could use personal items, such as hair, nail clippings, clothing, or even bodily waste, to work their dark magic against their targets. This belief was not unique only to Scotland; it was common in other parts of the world, including in Europe, Africa, South Asia, Polynesia, Melanesia, and North and South America. Another one of the sinister claims involving dark magic was that some witches would murder innocent children to obtain ingredients for their spells.

Conditions that we now recognize as postpartum psychosis were often mistaken for signs of witchcraft or black magic back in the medieval era. Because of this, women who displayed symptoms of mental distress or erratic behavior were sometimes accused of consorting with dark forces and the devil himself.

Witches were also believed to work in secret, often gathering at night when normal humans were sleeping. However, witches were said to be the most vulnerable while sleeping. They were also thought to transgress social norms by engaging in practices like cannibalism, incest, and open nudity. Some even claimed that witches had associations with certain animals, suggesting they could shape-shift into these creatures or had animal helpers to aid them in completing their sinister work.

Necromancy, the darkest of all black magic practices, was also attributed to witches. It involved communicating with the dead and summoning dark spirits. It was a terrifying idea that struck fear into the hearts of many.

However, it was possible to seek protection from the malicious powers of these evil witches. Referred to as "cunning folks," these special individuals were believed to possess the ability to cast protective spells. They were often sought after, especially if one wished to thwart a certain dark magic intended to harm them. Typically, charms, talismans, and amulets were the most common items used to safeguard themselves from witchcraft. Anti-witch marks, inscribed symbols or patterns, were sometimes carved into buildings to ward off evil magic. Witch bottles, which contained things like pins and urine, were buried to turn away curses. Additionally, items like horse skulls were sometimes concealed within the walls of buildings as protective symbols.

Once a person was sure they had been put under a witch's spell or a curse, they sought various means of release. Apart from consulting with the cunning folks, some believed that another cure for bewitchment was to persuade or force the alleged witch to lift their spell. However, in darker times, people attempted to thwart witchcraft by physically punishing the accused. Banishment, wounding, torture, and even execution were seen as ways to cleanse the community of this perceived evil.

This atmosphere of fear and paranoia led to a period in history known as the witch hunts. Many individuals, mostly women, were accused of witchcraft and subjected to trials that often ended in death. A majority of the time, accusations of witchcraft were a convenient scapegoat for any inconvenience or misfortune troubling a community. When plagues, diseases, famines, or other calamities struck, people pointed their fingers at supposed witches, blaming them for the afflictions and labeling them as agents of the devil.

The witch hunts in Scotland were a dark and troubling chapter in its history, marked by fear, paranoia, and the persecution of hundreds of innocent people. The roots of the Scottish witch hunts can be traced back to the reign of King James V.

As a young boy, King James V had been imprisoned by his stepfather, Archibald Douglas, 6th Earl of Angus. His escape from captivity left him with a burning desire for vengeance, not only against Douglas but also against his extended family, including his sister, Janet Douglas, Lady Glamis. In 1537, James arrested Janet, accusing her of witchcraft and concocting potions in a conspiracy to kill him.

The charges against Janet were largely founded on rumors and the desire for revenge. Even those who knew her were not safe; they were tortured mercilessly and forced to voice out any so-called evidence that could cement Janet's downfall. On July 17th, 1537, in a tragic and brutal event, Janet Douglas was burned alive on Castle Hill in Edinburgh, with her own son forced to watch the terrifying scene.

This event marked the beginning of a dark era in Scotland's history, where accusations of witchcraft became increasingly common and often led to gruesome outcomes. The paranoia surrounding witchcraft never subsided; instead, it only intensified as the years went by.

One of the most notorious episodes in the Scottish witch trials was the North Berwick witch trials in the late 16th century. King James VI, who was deeply superstitious and considered himself the devil's greatest mortal enemy, personally examined the accused individuals. He even wrote a book on the subject called *Daemonologie*, which further fueled the hysteria surrounding witchcraft.

An illustration of a witch trial in the 19ᵗʰ century.
https://commons.wikimedia.org/wiki/File:Punishment_of_Witches.png

In the North Berwick witch trials, a group of people, mainly women from East Lothian, were accused of meeting with the devil and conspiring to conjure storms that would kill King James VI and his wife, Queen Anne, upon their return from Denmark. As per usual, the accused were subjected to harsh interrogations and brutal torture, including sleep deprivation and other forms of torment, to extract confessions.

Women accused of witchcraft kneeling before King James during the North Berwick witch trials.

No one could live in peace during this traumatic time, not even the most innocent of all. The mere presence of birthmarks or unusual physical characteristics was often considered evidence of witchcraft. Many individuals were captured, tried, and executed under the suspicion of being witches.

Another notable witch hunt was the Great Scottish witch hunt of 1649-1650. The years leading up to this dark episode were far from peaceful. The people of Scotland were torn apart by religious and political conflicts and were deeply affected by the Wars of the Three Kingdoms. This turbulent atmosphere created fertile ground for accusations of witchcraft.

It was common to see people pointing fingers at each other, claiming they had made pacts with the devil and were capable of wielding dark powers to bring harm to their already distraught community. Fear and suspicion ran rampant. Families and friends were torn apart, as mistrust greatly festered in the hearts of the people.

To seek out these perceived threats, the Scottish Parliament appointed special commissioners known as "witch prickers." These individuals claimed to have the uncanny ability to identify witches through physical examinations. Oftentimes, they would meticulously examine the accused person's body for any unusual skin blemishes, moles, birthmarks, or other marks that they believed could be marks of the devil. Any irregularity in the skin could be interpreted as evidence of witchcraft. Witch prickers also used various sharp objects, such as needles, pins, or bodkins, to prick the accused person's skin. They believed that the devil's mark would be insensitive to pain and would not bleed when pricked.

Once accused, it was only a matter of seconds before unspeakable horrors took place. Sleep deprivation, binding, and even the dreaded "swimming" tests were used. In the swimming test, the accused would be stripped to their undergarments and bound, with their right thumb tied to their left big toe and their left thumb tied to their right big toe, to prevent them from swimming. They would then be lowered into a body of water. If the accused floated, they were deemed witches, as it was believed that the pure element of water rejected them due to their connection with the devil, and their fate was sealed. If they sank, they were considered innocent because the water had accepted them. However, they often met a tragic end beneath the water's surface if not rescued in time.

Religious leaders also played a significant role in fanning the flames of the witch hunts. A new Witchcraft Act was passed in 1649. Some ministers and clergymen preached sermons that reinforced the belief in witchcraft and the need to eradicate it. The religious fervor of the time only served to heighten the hysteria surrounding witch trials.

The Great Scottish witch hunt of 1649-1650 resulted in a significant number of executions. It is estimated that over three hundred individuals, mostly women of low social status, met their fate as witches during this dark period.

As time passed, the political landscape shifted, and the authorities turned their focus elsewhere. By the mid-1650s, the clamor for witch trials began to subside, though there were occasional local outbreaks from time to time. One tragic case that stands out during this period is that of Lilias Adie from the town of Torryburn in 1704. Accused of witchcraft, Lilias was subjected to brutal interrogation and torture. The relentless pressure eventually led her to confess to having interactions with the devil, attending meetings with other witches, and even engaging in carnal relations with the devil himself. The authorities pressed her to reveal the names of the other witches, but Lilias died before she could stand trial.

Since Lilias died before being formally convicted, her body could not be subjected to the gruesome fate of burning at the stake. However, the community remained convinced of her guilt and feared that the devil might reanimate her corpse. To prevent this, Lilias was buried in a peculiar manner—between the high and low tide marks on the beach, a place neither entirely land nor sea. A heavy stone slab was then added to her grave to ensure that her restless spirit would never get the chance to rise from the underworld.

The last recorded witch executions in Scotland occurred in 1706. The last trial took place in 1727. However, these dark episodes of unjust trials are never forgotten; instead, they serve as a somber lesson in history.

Acknowledging the wrongs done to those accused of being witches, the Scottish government formally apologized in 2022. Several memorials have been erected in remembrance of the victims. At Edinburgh Castle's esplanade, one can find the Witches Well, a monument to those who suffered during the witch hunts. The Fife Witches Trail also acts as a moving reminder of the stories and lives tragically altered by the fear and hysteria surrounding witchcraft.

Curses in Scottish Folktales

Although the old witch hunts are now part of history, the fear of curses remains for some people. Curses are thought to be spoken by powerful individuals, usually driven by emotions like anger, betrayal, or a wish for revenge. These curses are thought to hold the power to shape destinies, influence the future, and bring calamity upon those who invite their wrath.

The belief in curses often revolves around the idea that negative energy can be channeled through words or rituals, causing misfortune to befall the cursed individual or their descendants. Some curses are said to linger for generations, casting a shadow over entire families or even communities. One such story took place in the village of Lochbuie. This tale, recorded by the Scottish folklorist John Gregorson Campbell, tells the story of sisters, secrets, and the power of a curse.

According to the story, the older sister stood out for her beauty and kindness. Her charm and warmth drew the admiration of many, earning her the name Lovely Mairearad. Her sister, Ailsa, was smaller in size, though she possessed the same kindness as her elder sister. However, it was her ultimate devotion to Mairearad that earned Ailsa her nickname; she was often called by the villagers as Limpet Ailsa.

One day, a cheeky lad and his group of friends walked by and pestered Limpet Ailsa about Lovely Mairearad's affections. His endless questions pushed Ailsa to the brink, and she snapped, "My sister has a fairy lover, more handsome than any of you!" Laughter immediately erupted, but Ailsa, filled with annoyance, challenged them to visit their cottage at dusk.

The lads, drawn by the promise of entertainment, followed Ailsa. To their amazement, a real fairy appeared. The birds stopped singing, and the clouds stood still. Knowing the mortals had discovered him, he vanished as quickly as he appeared, leaving them in complete awe. Yet, Lovely Mairearad's response shattered their joy. She wailed, having warned Ailsa never to reveal her secret lest she be abandoned by her fairy lover.

From that day, Mairearad became a wandering soul, shunning houses and kind words. Desperate villagers tried to reconcile the two sisters, but all they heard were Mairearad's cruel curses, foretelling revenge upon Ailsa's descendants:

"If a fae indeed possesses an otherworldly power, get me my revenge, but may it be on her descendants."

Limpet Ailsa spent a year trying to mend their bond but had no success. She retreated to the north of the isle, where she married and had a son named Torquil, who inherited Mairearad's beauty and charm. Torquil possessed more than just his fair appearance; he was also known for his exceptional reaping skills. Some claimed he could reap as much as seven men could. Oftentimes, he would challenge the villagers during harvest time, boasting his talent as the best reaper in the area.

However, one day, a lady caught Torquil's attention. This mysterious woman, known among the villagers as the Maiden of the Cairn, possessed a reaping skill that matched Torquil's. Of course, Torquil, in his youthful pride, felt challenged by the mysterious lady. Thus, he picked up his sickle and joined her in the field, convinced that he could easily outdo her.

But as they toiled side by side, Torquil soon realized that the Maiden was no ordinary woman. She seemed to glide through the stalks of grain, her sickle moving with an otherworldly grace. Torquil struggled to keep up. His legs trembled, and his chest heaved with exhaustion.

Suddenly, in the midst of their reaping contest, the Maiden spoke words of warning.

"It is an evil thing, early on Monday, to reap the harvest maiden."

According to Scottish beliefs, the harvest maiden is a special doll, a representation of the last bundle of grain that marks the end of the harvest season in Scotland. But Torquil, in his eagerness, made a grave mistake. He cut the harvest maiden too soon. This act was seen as bad luck. It angered the spirits and magical beings believed to protect the crops. They took offense and unleashed their wrath upon Torquil.

And so, Torquil's life ended in the very field he aimed to conquer. The Maiden vanished, and Mairearad's wish, or rather curse, came true—her sister's family met a tragic end.

Of course, the world of curses is not confined to the distant past. Sometimes, it creeps into our lives, even in more recent times. Another chilling story took place sometime in the 1930s. It began with a well-respected Scottish baronet named Sir Alexander Seton and his wife, who embarked on a journey to Egypt, a land rich with ancient mysteries.

Their Egyptian adventure was said to have led them to the Temple of Luxor. Despite the strict prohibition against removing anything from the sacred tombs, Lady Seton could not resist the temptation. She quietly plucked a small bone as a memento, a token of their exotic travels, and brought it back to their grand home in Learmonth Gardens, Edinburgh. This mysterious—or rather cursed—piece of bone was displayed in a glass case stored in their lavish dining room. This seemingly innocent act inadvertently set in motion a series of events they would soon come to regret.

Upon their return, strange and unsettling occurrences began to unfold. Mysterious crashes reverberated through the house, and furniture was discovered in disarray as if moved by unseen hands. Ornaments lay shattered in rooms that had been empty mere moments before. Lady Seton herself fell suddenly and inexplicably ill, her ailment baffling even the most skilled doctors.

Time and time again, the family found themselves besieged by bizarre happenings that defied all explanation. But the most unsettling of all was the apparition that manifested itself in the house—an eerie figure cloaked in long robes. This ghostly presence appeared before multiple witnesses, both residents and visitors alike. The house's servants, overwhelmed by fear, desperately sought employment elsewhere, unwilling to endure the unnerving atmosphere another day.

In an attempt to rid themselves of this curse, Sir Alexander lent the bone to a scientist friend. To their astonishment, the ghostly disturbances ceased at Learmonth Gardens but resurfaced in the home of the scientist. The haunting stories soon reached the crowds, attracting the attention of even the newspapers of Edinburgh, which later dubbed the ghostly disturbances as the "The Curse of the Pharaoh."

In a bid to relieve his friend from the torment, Sir Alexander Seton reclaimed the bone and returned it to Learmonth Gardens. Once more, the house seemed to come alive with inexplicable phenomena. Even Sir Alexander himself fell ill.

In the end, seeking solace and deliverance, Sir Alexander turned to a priest. The bone was unearthed, and in a ritual of purifying fire, it was reduced to ashes. With the bone's destruction, the curse was finally lifted, and the tormented house was freed from its malevolent grip.

Chapter 8: Love and Betrayal: The Sagas of Scotland

In addition to stories of magical creatures and malicious beings intervening in the lives of mortals, Scottish folklore is deeply cherished for its love stories and sagas. These tales, which often weaved together the themes of beauty, tragedy, and destiny, strike a chord with the Scots, reflecting their fondness for stories that mirror the complexities of the human heart and the dramatic landscapes that surround them. One such tale that was passed from one generation to the next is that of Deirdre, set during the reign of Conchobar, the king of Ulster.

It began in Ireland when the king attended a feast at the house of Felimid the Harper. Amidst the celebration, an incident occurred that led the druid Cathbad to make a prophecy about Felimid's unborn daughter, Deirdre. Cathbad foretold that Deirdre would grow up to be a woman of unparalleled beauty. Felimid and his wife were overjoyed upon hearing this, but their expressions immediately changed when the druid made another remark.

"But anything excessive never brings good. True, your daughter will be the fairest of all, but her life will also be marked by tragedy and sorrow. Our people will soon be divided. Brothers will fight each other, hoping they can win dear Deirdre's affection."

Upon listening to Cathbad's words, the men of the Red Branch, the elite warriors of Ulster, feared the chaos Deirdre's beauty might bring and demanded that the child be killed. However, King Conchobar, who always desired to be seen as a wise and merciful ruler, refused. He declared that he would take the child upon her birth and raise her in secret. If she did grow into the beauty Cathbad predicted, Conchobar declared that he would marry her, placing her in a position so high that no man would dare look upon her.

And so, true to the prophecy, Deirdre was born with a beauty that promised to eclipse all others. And just as Conchobar had planned, she was placed under the care of a nurse named Leabharcham and hidden away in a secluded valley, far from the prying eyes of the world. There, Deirdre grew up under Leabharcham's protective watch, completely isolated from the outside world. Conchobar was curious about his future bride and made periodic visits to check on her. No one else was allowed to see Deirdre except an old man who tended to the valley. However, the old man was mute, so the secret of her existence remained safe.

The tale took a dramatic turn one fateful day. As Deirdre neared womanhood, an incident sparked a deep longing in her heart. Leabharcham had the old man slaughter a calf. The calf's blood spilled on the snow, drawing a raven to the scene. Deirdre, who had been watching the incident from a close distance, was said to be overly captivated by the contrast of the raven's black feathers against the blood-red snow and the pure white ground. This moment led to a sudden realization. She proclaimed that she would fall in love only with a man who had hair as black as the raven's feathers, skin as white as the pure snow, and cheeks as red as the blood on the snow.

Longing for love, Deirdre asked her caretaker if she knew any man who fit her description. Leabharcham was hesitant at first, but she could never ignore Deirdre for too long. The protective caretaker informed her of one particular man who went by the name Naoise. However, Leabharcham strictly warned her to only observe the man from a distance. After all, he was one of the three sons of Uisneach, who were renowned warriors of high status. Deirdre was raised to believe that she was a commoner. Such a union could attract significant attention and potential danger.

An early 20th-century painting of Deirdre.

Deirdre agreed to this. So, one day, she hid amidst the bushes, eyeing Naoise and his brothers from afar. The moment she laid eyes on the man, Deirdre knew he was the embodiment of her heart's desire. Enthralled, she completely forgot about her promise. She leaped out of her hiding spot and confronted Naoise, pleading for him to run away with her. Naoise, who knew that Deirdre was supposed to marry King Conchobar, initially refused her request, but Deirdre already had a plan in mind. She put a geis—a compelling magical vow—on Naoise, binding him to her will.

Deirdre and Naoise, along with his brothers, fled to Scotland. They lived a secluded life deep in the woods, away from the eyes of the world and especially the Ulster king, who was furious with their elopement. Naoise and his brothers swore service under the Scottish king, but Deirdre soon realized the king coveted her for himself. Knowing that he could not kill the brothers outright, the Scottish king placed the brothers on the front lines of every battle, hoping they would eventually fall. However, their prowess as warriors kept them safe. Deirdre, seeing the danger, persuaded Naoise to flee farther into the wilderness. They eventually settled on a remote island near the training school of the warrior woman Scathach and lived there for many years.

Back in the Ulster capital, Emain Macha, Fergus Mac Roich, a noble of the Red Branch, was the only one brave enough to speak of the sons of Uisneach to Conchobar. Despite Conchobar's rage whenever Naoise's betrayal was mentioned, Fergus, who was fond of the brothers, argued tirelessly for their forgiveness. Eventually, Conchobar relented, allowing Fergus to invite them back under his protection.

So, without delay, Fergus journeyed to Scotland and shared the joyous news with the brothers. They were thrilled at the prospect of returning to Emain Macha and swore an oath not to eat or sleep until they were home. However, during the voyage back, Deirdre grieved for the Scottish lands she had grown to love, singing a lament for the mountains and lochs that had been her haven.

Unbeknownst to Fergus and the brothers, King Conchobar was not ready to let the past go. Fergus Mac Roich had long been under a geis, where he was prohibited from refusing an invitation to a feast of ale. King Conchobar was aware of this vulnerability, and he cunningly invited Fergus to a drinking session, forcing him to abandon his duty to protect Deirdre and the sons of Uisneach. Deirdre, already anxious about their return to Ulster, grew increasingly wary. She implored Fergus not to desert them, accusing him of cowardice for abandoning the men under his protection. Unfortunately, bound by his geis, Fergus had no choice but to attend the feast. He did, however, entrust the safety of Deirdre and the sons of Uisneach to his son Fiachu before departing.

So, the journey continued. Upon reaching Emain Macha, they were greeted not by King Conchobar but by Leabharcham, Deirdre's former caretaker. Ever protective of Deirdre, Leabharcham advised Naoise to hide Deirdre's beauty from prying eyes, hoping none would notice her return. Conchobar, still struggling with his feelings for Deirdre, eventually inquired about her appearance. Leabharcham chose to lie to the king, describing her as a haggard shadow of her former self.

Initially, Conchobar believed Leabharcham's words, and his jealousy waned, replaced by a desire to reintegrate the sons of Uisneach into his service. However, he soon doubted Leabharcham's claim, as he knew the caretaker would do anything to shield her ward from harm. So, to discover the truth, the king sent a spy to ascertain Deirdre's true appearance. Once the spy returned, he confirmed that Deirdre remained the most beautiful woman in Ireland. Conchobar's jealousy and anger were reignited, leading him to order an attack against Naoise and his brothers.

The Red Branch hesitated. While some obeyed the king, others refused to turn against their former comrades. Nevertheless, a battle took place. In the ensuing chaos, Fiachu Mac Roigh, son of Fergus, fought bravely against Conchobar Mac Neasa's son in single combat. Fiachu fell during the duel, and Conchobar's son met his demise soon afterward.

Seeing his men faltering, Conchobar sought the aid of Cathbad the druid. Cathbad agreed to help under one condition: Conchobar was to promise not to kill the sons of Uisneach. Conchobar agreed, declaring he only sought an apology from Naoise. Thus, with the druid's help, the tide of the battle turned. However, Conchobar, bound by his promise to Cathbad, used Maigne Rough Hand, the son of the king of Norway, to execute his vengeance. In the end, Naoise and his brothers met their fate; all three were beheaded by Maigne Rough Hand.

Upon learning that she would never see the love of her life ever again, Deidre immediately plunged into despair. She refused Conchobar's advances despite his attempts to court her with wealth and status. After a year of her steadfast refusal, Conchobar grew irritated. So, he devised a cruel plan. He first asked Deirdre who she despised more than him, to which she replied, Maigne Rough Hand, Naoise's killer. Seizing on this, Conchobar decided to give Deirdre to Maigne for a year, suggesting that Maigne could do anything he wished to her.

"Let's see if you change your mind about me once he gets his hands on you," Conchobar said.

Deirdre was sent away in Maigne's chariot. However, Deirdre had one last act of defiance to display. As the chariot passed a cliff, Deirdre was said to have leaned out and dashed her head against the rocks, ending her own life.

Deirdre was laid to rest in Emain Macha, close to the graves of Naoise and his brothers. In a final act of spite, Conchobar placed wooden stakes between the two lovers' graves, intending to separate them even after death. However, nature had its own plan. These stakes eventually took root and grew into two trees that intertwined, symbolizing the everlasting love between Deirdre and Naoise, a love that not even death nor the envy of a king could keep apart.

Thomas the Rhymer and the Queen of Elfland

While it is pretty common for love tales to end tragically, the story of Thomas the Rhymer and the Queen of Elfland breaks this mold in a captivating way. It is a tale not of sorrow and loss but of wonder, deep connection, and a love that transcends the boundaries of different worlds.

Some believe that Thomas the Rhymer was a real person, although it would be safer to call him a semi-legendary figure (a real person whose life story mainly lies in the realm of myth). He is said to have lived in the 13th century. His early life is shrouded in mystery, but it is safe to assume that he was just an ordinary man—at least before his encounter with the majestic Fae. This particular story began in the town of Erceldoune amidst the rolling hills close to the Scottish Borders. Thomas's heart yearned for the poetry of the natural world, and he often wandered the countryside. He could be seen by his fellow villagers taking a quiet stroll along the riverbed, his steps guided by the whispers of the wind and the peaceful songs of the streams.

On one fine day, perhaps slightly tired after exploring nature, Thomas found himself resting beneath an ancient tree. Its branches were heavy with blossoms—it was the beginning of spring. The tree was known by many as the Eildon Tree. Here, Thomas sat for hours. He was lost in his thoughts, his mind playing around with poetry and verse. It was then that Thomas suddenly felt a change in his surroundings. The air around Thomas shimmered with a strange, ethereal light, and the sound of silver bells danced upon the breeze.

Thomas the Rhymer and the Queen of Elfland's first encounter.
https://commons.wikimedia.org/wiki/File:Katherine_Cameron-Thomas_the_Rhymer.png

From the heart of this otherworldly glow emerged a vision that transcended the bounds of mortal comprehension. A horse, white as milk or even snow, bore upon its back a lady of such resplendent beauty that it seemed the very essence of the forest had taken form. Dressed in a gown of the deepest green and adorned with jewels that sparkled like dewdrops under the morning sun, she was a vision of enchantment. This was no mortal maiden but the Queen of Elfland herself.

Their eyes met, and in that gaze, a connection deeper than time itself was forged. Thomas was enraptured by her ethereal grace and felt his heart drawn to her as if by an invisible thread. The Queen, sensing the purity of his spirit, offered him a choice: journey into the unknown realms of Elfland in exchange for a kiss or do nothing and continue with his life, which would be forever unmarked by the wonders beyond. With a heart full of longing and a soul captivated by love, Thomas chose the path of the Fae. Without hesitation, he rose to his feet and kissed the otherworldly queen.

As soon as he made his choice, they journeyed to Elfland, a place where time moves differently. Days feel like years, and years pass in a moment. The Queen showed Thomas around this enchanting world, teaching him secrets and knowledge no mortal has ever known. Thomas was undoubtedly enchanted, as he was given a chance to see wonders beyond imagination—some he only heard when he was young in tales told by his elders.

However, fate and destiny had other plans for the two lovers. Their time together was bound by rules not of their making. Some claimed that every seven years, the fairies had to pay a tribute to darker forces. The Queen, fearing that Thomas might be the price of this grim levy, could not bear the thought of losing her beloved to such a fate. In a decision torn between love and duty, she chose to return him to the world of mortals.

Another tale spoke of a different reason for Thomas's return. It was said that the Queen, seeking to shield their love from the prying eyes of the Fairy King, sent Thomas back to Erceldoune. Their love was to remain hidden, a treasure known only to the hearts that bore it.

Whichever the reason, Thomas returned to the realm of humans under the same Eildon Tree. However, the Fairy Queen did not bid her goodbye without a gift. Thomas left the world of the Fae with a tongue that could not lie. Thomas could utter prophecies, and they would always be true. While some saw this ability as a blessing, others saw it as a burden.

Among his many predictions, Thomas foretold the death of King Alexander III, which led to the Wars of Scottish Independence. He spoke of a future where Scotland and England would unite under one crown, a prophecy realized centuries later with the accession of James VI of Scotland to the English throne. Thomas's visions extended beyond political realms, weaving tales of both love and loss.

Indeed, his gift brought him fame, but deep inside, he cherished the memories of Elfland and his time with the Queen more than anything. What happened to Thomas years later remains a mystery. Some say that Thomas was called back to the magical land and lives there still. Others believe he waits in secret, ready to return when Scotland needs him most.

Unlike other tragic love stories from that time, the tale of Thomas and the Queen did not end in sorrow. Instead, it lives on as a narrative of enduring love, magical adventure, and the idea that, even in a world steeped in tragedy, there can still be stories of wonder and hope.

Chapter 9: Sacred Sites

Much like its Celtic cousins—Ireland, Wales, and England—Scotland is home to various sacred sites. These sites are more than just monuments of stone and earth. They are also the silent witnesses to the land's colorful history and the still keepers of its deepest, mysterious, and enchanting secrets—be it of ancient kings, mythical creatures, or saintly miracles. From the enigmatic standing stones in the middle of nowhere to the hauntingly beautiful abbeys and eerie tombs, each site is a direct portal to a past that feels almost otherworldly. These places are important to properly understand Scotland's cultural identity, as they serve as reminders of a time when the natural world was revered and the veil between the earthly realm and the ethereal world was supposedly thin.

The Callanish Standing Stones

One of the most fascinating of these places is the Callanish Standing Stones. These towering stones, located on the Isle of Lewis in the Outer Hebrides, are a magnificent spectacle.

The history of the Callanish Stones is as deep and complex as the roots of the heather that blankets the Scottish moors. Erected around 2900 BCE, these megaliths predate Stonehenge. They are thought to have been placed by the hands of ancient people. The reasons why are lost to time, but the stones continue to fascinate us. However, for many centuries, the stones were concealed under a thick layer of peat turf and were only rediscovered in 1857.

The Callanish Stones during sunset.

The stones rise up against the skyline, tall and stoic. The standing stones measure at around twelve feet each and are arranged in a cruciform pattern around a central monolith of fourteen feet. They are made of Lewisian gneiss, a complex crystalline rock among the oldest in the world, dating back 1.7 to 3 billion years. These stones have witnessed numerous changing of skies and seasons. Some say this stone circle resembles an ancient gathering of wise men, forever locked in silent conversation.

The chambered tomb within the Callanish Standing Stones.

The tales and myths surrounding the Callanish Standing Stones are as interesting as the stones themselves. One popular legend, capturing the mystical nature of the site, tells of the stones being petrified giants who refused to convert to Christianity and were punished by Saint Kieran. Another enchanting story involves a magical white cow with red ears that mysteriously emerged from the sea to provide milk to the islanders during a time of need. Sadly, the cow's kindness was cut short due to the greed of a particular visitor. The cow disappeared, never to be seen again.

According to archaeological findings, these stone formations were probably central to various rituals during the Bronze Age. Historians believe that the site was in use for at least a millennium before being abandoned around 1000 BCE. The most accepted theory today is that these megaliths functioned as an astronomical observatory or a calendar based on celestial events. It's believed that the arrangement of the stones aligns with the movement of the moon, particularly during the lunar standstill, which occurs every 18.6 years.

It is also widely believed that the stones were related to the agricultural calendar, perhaps marking important events like the solstice or the equinox. However, today, the site attracts those who seek a connection with the past or wish to celebrate ancient traditions. During solstices, people often gather on the site to watch the sunrise or sunset, with the sun aligning with the stones in a mesmerizing display of light and shadow.

The Isle of Iona

Nestled in the embrace of the Atlantic Ocean, right off the western coast of Scotland, lies a small yet profoundly significant isle known as Iona. This sacred island measures just three miles long and a mile wide. Iona is also so remote that the only way to reach this island from either Edinburgh or Glasgow is through a train ride, two ferry journeys, and a scenic bus ride. However, the island is often regarded as a beacon of spiritual and historical significance for centuries. Unlike the millennia-old Callanish Standing Stones, Iona's allure lies in its serene beauty and its rich Christian and Celtic history.

Iona's story begins in the mists of time, with its first inhabitants arriving in the late Neolithic era. However, the isle truly came into prominence in 563 CE with the arrival of Saint Columba from Ireland. Saint Columba, or Colum Cille, was not only a monk but also a noble and a poet. He established a monastic community on Iona, which soon became a center for the spread of Christianity throughout Scotland and beyond. The monastery he founded served as a religious center and as a seat of learning, attracting scholars and religious figures from across Europe.

Panoramic view of Iona.
https://commons.wikimedia.org/wiki/File:TyIona20030825r17f31.jpg

The island's monastery rapidly grew in fame and importance, becoming a renowned center for art and learning in the Celtic world. It was here that the famous Book of Kells, an illuminated manuscript containing the four Gospels of the New Testament, is believed to have been created by the monks of Iona in the 8th century. This masterpiece of Christian art showcases the deep spiritual and artistic heritage of the island.

Despite being a center of both learning and religion, Iona was not excluded from the violence of war. Throughout the centuries, Iona saw its own share of turbulence. It was once raided by the Vikings in 795 CE and then suffered several political power struggles. Nevertheless, the island remained a sacred site.

Of course, legends and tales also exist in Iona. The prominent one tells of Saint Columba's encounter with an angel on the island who showed him a vision of heaven. This encounter is said to have deeply affected the saint, influencing his teachings and writings.

Another story speaks of the "Street of the Dead," a path along which the bodies of kings and chieftains were carried to be laid to rest. It is also believed that Macbeth, the Scottish king made famous by Shakespeare, was buried here, along with many other rulers from Scotland, Ireland, and even Norway.

The Abbey on Iona.

With its lush green hills that softly slope down to meet the soft, white sandy beaches and the vast expanse of the blue ocean, Iona offers a feeling of tranquility and reflection. The soothing sound of the waves and the calls of seabirds are usually the only things that disturb the profound quietness that surrounds the island.

As one walks the ancient paths of Iona, past the abbey and the ruins of a nunnery, there is a palpable sense of walking through history. The island is, more or less, a living museum, where each stone and every turn of the path tells a story of faith, art, and the enduring human spirit. It remains a place of pilgrimage, attracting those who seek solace, inspiration, and a deeper connection with the divine. To this day, the isle continues to be a shining jewel in Scotland's crown of sacred sites.

Arthur's Seat in Edinburgh

Believe it or not, Arthur's Seat, Edinburgh's most treasured mythic mountain, is actually an ancient volcano that last erupted about 340 million years ago. It has since eroded and glaciated to its current size. Standing at about 251 meters high, this extinct volcano gifts us with a panoramic view of the city and a journey into some of the most popular legends of Scotland. The history of Arthur's Seat is indeed as old as the rocks that form it, dating back hundreds of millions of years ago.

Arthur's Seat.

However, how exactly the site got its name is shrouded in legend. Some say it is named after the legendary King Arthur, suggesting that it was one of the possible locations for Camelot, the legendary castle and court of the famous king. Others suggest that the dormant volcano had another name and that it was derived from a Gaelic phrase. Back when Holyrood Park was a royal hunting ground, an archer set a record for the longest arrow shot in the kingdom. His arrow was said to have flown an impressive 251 meters from the hunting area to the summit of the hill now known as Arthur's Seat. Since then, the locals started calling the hill "Àrd-na-Saighead" or "Height of Arrows" in recognition of this feat.

Arthur's Seat holds a few intriguing tales. One story tells us of a ferocious dragon known for terrorizing the old town of Edinburgh. Some say this tale predates even Celtic times. According to the age-old legend, the dragon never knew how to rest. Every day, the malicious creature would circle the sky, snatching and devouring any animals it came across, including the locals' livestock. The people of Edinburgh were beyond terrified of the dragon, especially when they did not know how to satisfy its never-ending greed. And so, the creature ate and plagued the humble lands continuously for years. However, in the end, it was its own greed that eventually led to the dragon's demise.

The dragon was believed to have grown extremely fat. Laziness took over the creature, and it no longer attacked the towns and villages. One day, the dragon flew to the hill just outside of Edinburgh. Perhaps exhausted from its daily excursions, the creature rested on the summit. Unfortunately for the gigantic dragon, that was the last time it ever flew again. As the legend goes, the dragon lay down to rest and fell into a deep slumber from which it never awoke. Over time, the dragon's massive body turned to stone, its curves and contours forming the hills and crags that now make up the landscape of Arthur's Seat.

Arthur's Seat is fascinating in regards to actual history as well. Archaeological finds, including a fort on the summit dating back to around 600 CE, suggest that it was an important site for early settlers. Perhaps the most intriguing mystery surrounding the extinct volcano emerged in 1836 with the discovery of miniature coffins.

A group of young boys were hunting for rabbits, and they stumbled upon a small cave on the northeastern slopes of Arthur's Seat. Inside this cave, they found something unexpected and startling: a collection of seventeen tiny coffins, each carefully carved and containing a small wooden figure dressed in custom-made clothes. The figures, which appeared to be dressed in a style resembling funeral attire, were meticulously crafted, with attention to detail that spoke of a deliberate and purposeful act.

The discovery of these miniature coffins set off a wave of speculation and theories about their origin and purpose. Some thought they were involved in witchcraft or were tokens to ward off evil spirits. Others speculated that they were connected to the infamous Burke and Hare murders, suggesting that the coffins represented each of the murderers' victims, though records claim that the murderers killed sixteen victims. This theory, though widely discussed, has little evidence to support it.

Another theory suggests that these coffins were created as a form of memorial, perhaps for sailors lost at sea. The attention to detail in the clothes and the careful arrangement of the coffins might indicate a grieving process or a tribute to the deceased.

The Clava Cairns

Near the banks of the River Nairn lies Clava Cairns, another site as mysterious as it is ancient. This complex of burial cairns and standing stones, dating back to the Bronze Age, about four thousand years ago, offers a fascinating glimpse into Scotland's prehistoric past. Unlike the vibrant tales of Arthur's Seat or the spiritual resonance of the Isle of Iona, Clava Cairns exudes an aura of ancient solemnity and profound mystique.

The Clava Cairns.

Nachosan, CC BY-SA 3.0 <https://creativecommons.org/licenses/by-sa/3.0>, via Wikimedia Commons: https://commons.wikimedia.org/wiki/File:Clava_cairn_(Balnauran_of_Clava)_28.JPG

Clava Cairns, also known as the Balnuaran of Clava, consists of a group of well-preserved burial cairns surrounded by standing stones. The site is divided into two types of cairns: passage cairns and ring cairns. The passage cairns, with their narrow passageways leading to central chambers, were likely used for burials, while the ring cairns, which have no apparent entrance, might have served a different ceremonial purpose.

The cairns are constructed with remarkable precision. Each one is surrounded by a circle of standing stones, with some stones positioned to align with the movements of the sun, particularly during the winter solstice. This alignment suggests that the site was not only a burial place but also a ceremonial space where ancient people might have celebrated and marked the changing of the seasons.

The stones themselves are a source of wonder. Made of a local variety of split stones known as whinstone, they range in height and shape, with some featuring mysterious cup and ring marks. These carvings might have held ritual significance; they were possibly used in ceremonies or as a way to mark ownership or heritage.

Legends and folklore are deeply entwined with Clava Cairns. One popular claim tells of spirits that guard the sacred site, protecting the ancient secrets buried within. Some even warned outsiders not to remain at the site during nighttime since the cairns hold mysteries that are beyond our mortal comprehension. About two decades ago, Clava Cairns was said to have inflicted a curse upon a Belgian tourist when he took a piece of a stone at the site as a souvenir. Little did he know, this tiny piece of memento brought havoc to his household, and he desperately sent the stone to a tourist office in Inverness, along with a letter explaining the incidents that had occurred. According to his writings, ever since he had brought the stone home, his family only knew misfortunes. His daughter broke her leg, his wife got mysteriously ill, and the man broke his arm and lost his job.

Mythic and peculiar incidents aside, the solitude and atmosphere of Clava Cairns are striking. Tucked away in a quiet grove, the site exudes a sense of uninterrupted time, offering a palpable connection to the distant past. Visitors often report a sense of awe and peace, as if stepping into a different world where time stands still and the modern world's noise fades away.

In recent years, Clava Cairns has gained international attention through its association with the popular *Outlander* series, as it inspired the fictional Craigh Na Dun, a place of time travel. This connection has brought new visitors who are eager to experience the mystical allure of the cairns for themselves.

The Whithorn Priory

The history of Whithorn Priory is deeply entwined with the spread of Christianity in Scotland. Founded around 397 CE by Saint Ninian, the first known Christian missionary to Scotland, the priory is considered one of the earliest centers of Christian worship in the country. Saint Ninian established a church at Whithorn, known as Candida Casa (White House), which allowed him to evangelize the surrounding regions. This church, the first stone-built church in Scotland, marked the beginning of a tradition of Christian worship and pilgrimage that has lasted for centuries.

Saint Ninian's chapel.

The priory, whose ruins remain today, was established much later, around the 12th century. It became a site of significant religious and cultural importance, drawing pilgrims from across Scotland and beyond. The priory was home to a community of monks who followed the Premonstratensian order, which was known for its commitment to piety and learning.

Whithorn became a focal point for pilgrims, partly due to the belief that Saint Ninian was buried there. Pilgrims journeyed to the site, seeking spiritual solace, healing, and blessings. One prominent pilgrim was Robert the Bruce. In 1329, toward the end of his life and suffering from a serious illness, Robert the Bruce made a pilgrimage to Whithorn. He sought healing and perhaps divine favor at the shrine of Saint Ninian. Despite his faith and the hope for a miracle, Robert the Bruce succumbed to his illness three months after his visit.

Whithorn Priory, the nave of the cathedral.

David II, Robert the Bruce's son, also made an important pilgrimage to Whithorn. Legend says that during the Battle of Neville's Cross in 1346, David II was hit by two arrows. One of these arrows could not be removed. However, after a pilgrimage to Whithorn's shrine, the arrow was finally taken out successfully.

The significance of Whithorn Priory extends beyond its religious history. It was a center of learning and culture, with monks playing a vital role in the preservation and production of religious texts and artifacts. Today, the site's ruins, including the Priory Church, offer a glimpse into its grand past.

Whithorn has also seen a revival of pilgrimage in recent years. The Whithorn Way, a modern pilgrimage route, allows visitors to follow in the footsteps of medieval pilgrims, journeying through the stunning landscapes of southwestern Scotland to the historic site. This contemporary pilgrimage experience connects people with the rich spiritual heritage of Whithorn, blending past and present in a journey of reflection and discovery.

Conclusion

As we travel through the misty highlands and deep lochs of Scotland's mythological landscape, we are constantly reminded of the profound influence these ancient tales hold in shaping the nation's culture, identity, and storytelling tradition. This book has been a voyage across time, delving into a variety of tales, characters, and themes. These stories are not only central to Scottish mythology but have also continued to resonate deeply with modern audiences, both young and old alike.

Scottish mythology's continued appeal lies in its ability to speak to the human condition and to explore the depths of our fears, desires, and hopes. These ancient stories remind us of our connection to the past, to the land, and to the shared human experiences that transcend time and place. They are more than just tales; they are a window into the soul of a nation, reflecting the values, beliefs, and aspirations of the Scottish people.

The lasting impact of Scotland's mythological heritage is clear in modern culture, arts, and literature. These ancient narratives, filled with heroism, romance, tragedy, and the supernatural, have stood the test of time, inspiring numerous creative works. In films and television shows, elements of Scottish myths are often woven into narratives, creating worlds filled with magic and wonder. For instance, the allure of the Scottish Highlands, haunted by the spirits of its past and the legends of its people, has captivated filmmakers, leading to cinematic portrayals that paint the nation's myths and history in a new light.

In literature, the influence of Scottish mythology is equally profound. Novels, both historical and fantasy, frequently draw upon the rich well of

Celtic lore, reimagining old tales or embedding mythological themes within new stories. Characters like the 13th-century Scottish leader William Wallace, mythical creatures such as kelpies and the Loch Ness Monster, and historical events, such as the witch hunts, have found new life in pages and screens, enchanting a new generation of readers and viewers worldwide.

Music, too, has been touched by these ancient narratives. Traditional Scottish music often encapsulates the essence of these myths, with ballads telling tales of love, loss, and adventure. Contemporary musicians continue to draw inspiration from these stories, using them to create songs that speak of the land's ancient past and the timeless human experiences reflected in these myths.

The reinterpretation of classic legends and the incorporation of mythological themes in new works are not just acts of creativity; they're proof of the lasting importance of these stories. They serve as bridges connecting the past with the present, keeping the essence of Scottish mythology vibrant in our shared awareness.

As we look to the future, there is hope that these captivating stories will continue to be cherished, shared, and reimagined. It is essential that Scotland's mythological wisdom, values, and heritage remain a vital part of the nation's cultural legacy. In a world that is rapidly changing, these myths offer a link to the past, grounding us in tradition while inspiring new stories and interpretations.

If you enjoyed this book, a review on Amazon would be greatly appreciated because it would mean a lot to hear from you.

To leave a review:

1. Open your camera app.
2. Point your mobile device at the QR code.
3. The review page will appear in your web browser.

_____

Thanks for your support!

Here's another book by Enthralling History that you might like

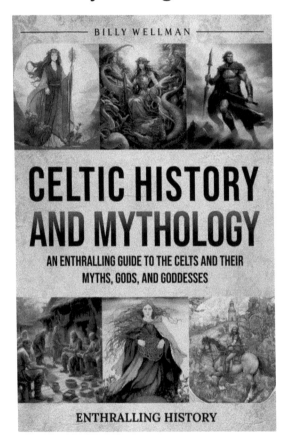

Free limited time bonus

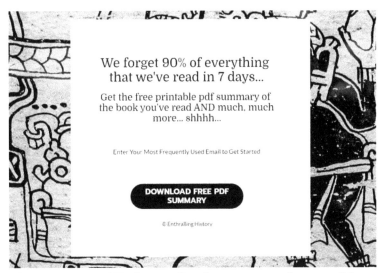

Stop for a moment. We have a free bonus set up for you. The problem is this: we forget 90% of everything that we read after 7 days. Crazy fact, right? Here's the solution: we've created a printable, 1-page pdf summary for this book that you're reading now. All you have to do to get your free pdf summary is to go to the following website: **https://livetolearn.lpages.co/enthrallinghistory/**

Or, Scan the QR code!

Once you do, it will be intuitive. Enjoy, and thank you!

Bibliography

"The Battle of Stirling Bridge." *National Wallace Monument*, https://www.nationalwallacemonument.com/the-battle-of-stirling-bridge/. Accessed 8 November 2023.

Buxton, Neil. "Economic Growth in Scotland between the wars." *The Economic History Review*, vol. 33, no. 4, 1980, pp. 538-55. *JSTOR*.

Clarkson, Tim. *The Picts: A History*. Birlinn, Limited, 2016.

"Edmund Cartwright | Lemelson." *Lemelson-MIT*, https://lemelson.mit.edu/resources/edmund-cartwright. Accessed 4 December 2023.

Herman, Arthur. *How the Scots Invented the Modern World: The True Story of How Western Europe's Poorest Nation Created Our World & Everything In It*. MJF Books, 2001.

Lira, Carl. "Watt Biography." *MSU College of Engineering*, https://www.egr.msu.edu/~lira/supp/steam/wattbio.html. Accessed 4 December 2023.

Maclean, Fitzroy, and Magnus Linklater. *Scotland: a concise history*. Thames & Hudson, 2000.

Morris, William Edward, and Charlotte R. Brown. "David Hume (Stanford Encyclopedia of Philosophy)." *Stanford Encyclopedia of Philosophy*, 26 February 2001, https://plato.stanford.edu/entries/hume/#LifeWork. Accessed 26 November 2023.

"North Berwick harbour severely damaged by huge waves." *BBC*, 30 October 2023, https://www.bbc.com/news/uk-scotland-edinburgh-east-fife-67259624. Accessed 30 October 2023.

"Scotland's People and the First World War." *National Records of Scotland*, https://www.nrscotland.gov.uk/research/learning/first-world-war/scotlands-people-and-the-first-world-war. Accessed 12 December 2023.

"Scots abroad: medical influences in the 18th century." *Royal College of Physicians of Edinburgh*, https://www.rcpe.ac.uk/heritage/scots-abroad-medical-influences-18th-century. Accessed 7 December 2023.

T, Milan, and Ellen Castelow. "Sir Walter Scott, his Life and Works." *Historic UK*, https://www.historic-uk.com/HistoryUK/HistoryofScotland/Sir-Walter-Scott/. Accessed 4 December 2023.

"WW1 Battalions." *The Royal Scots*, https://www.theroyalscots.co.uk/ww1-battalions/. Accessed 12 December 2023.

Brown, C. (2022, May 18). The Callanish Standing Stones: Stonehenge of the North. Good Nature Travel Blog | Stories Are Made on Adventures.

https://www.nathab.com/blog/callanish-standing-stones/

Brown, R. (2023, April 5). The Two Sisters and the Curse. Folklore Scotland. https://folklorescotland.com/the-two-sisters-and-the-curse/

By The Newsroom. (2016, April 19). Five parts of Scotland you didn't know were cursed. The Scotsman. https://www.scotsman.com/whats-on/arts-and-entertainment/five-parts-of-scotland-you-didnt-know-were-cursed-1478389

By The Newsroom. (2016, April 19). Five parts of Scotland you didn't know were cursed. The Scotsman. https://www.scotsman.com/whats-on/arts-and-entertainment/five-parts-of-scotland-you-didnt-know-were-cursed-1478389

By The Newsroom. (2016, October 25). Was tourist cursed by sacred Highland site? The Scotsman. https://www.scotsman.com/whats-on/arts-and-entertainment/was-tourist-cursed-by-sacred-highland-site-613927

Cameron, E. (2019, March 6). Legends of Argyll — Eilidh Cameron Photography. Eilidh Cameron Photography. https://www.eilidhcameronphotography.com/blog/2019/3/6/legends-of-argyll

Cartwright, M. (2023). Lugh. World History Encyclopedia. https://www.worldhistory.org/Lugh/#google_vignette

Deirdre of the Sorrows – Bard Mythologies. (n.d.). https://bardmythologies.com/deirdre-of-the-sorrows/

Facts, legend & History | Callanish (Calanais) Standing Stones. (2023, December 18). Calanais. https://calanais.org/explore/

Fairnie, R. (2019, October 29). Bone-chilling story behind Craigleith house "haunted" by ancient Egyptian mummy. Edinburgh Live. https://www.edinburghlive.co.uk/news/edinburgh-news/bone-chilling-story-behind-craigleith-17162657

Graeme. (2023, November 21). Scottish Witch Stories: The Facts & The Fiction. Scotland's Stories. https://scotlands-stories.com/scottish-witch-stories/

Great Castles - Lady Ghosts of Crathes Castle. (n.d.). https://great-castles.com/crathesghost.html

Great Castles - Lady Ghosts of Crathes Castle. (n.d.). https://great-castles.com/crathesghost.html

Hale, R. (2023, August 7). Hermitage Castle, Scotland's Fortress Of Nightmares | Spooky Isles. Spooky Isles. https://www.spookyisles.com/hermitage-castle/#google_vignette

Haunted Rooms. (2023, January 31). The Ghosts of Mary King's Close, Edinburgh | Haunted Rooms. Haunted Rooms. https://www.hauntedrooms.co.uk/mary-kings-close

IrishCentral Staff. (2023, March 21). The legendary "Deirdre of the Sorrows" and the Celtic tale's legacy. IrishCentral.com.

https://www.irishcentral.com/roots/legendary-deirdre-sorrows+

Jackcairney. (2022, July 7). Legends from the Old Man of Storr - Hidden Scotland. Hidden Scotland. https://hiddenscotland.co/legends-from-the-old-man-of-storr/#:~:text=Some%20say%20the%20Old%20Man,their%20long%20and%20happy%20marriage

Jackcairney. (2022, July 7). Legends from the Old Man of Storr - Hidden Scotland. Hidden Scotland. https://hiddenscotland.co/legends-from-the-old-man-of-storr/

Jewelry, S. I. (2023, May 5). The Legend of the Selkies: A Love & Transformation story. ShanOre Irish Jewelry. https://www.shanore.com/blog/the-legend-of-the-selkies/

Kingshill, S., & Westwood, J. (2009). The Lore of Scotland: A guide to Scottish legends. https://openlibrary.org/books/OL25081911M/The_lore_of_Scotland

Mark, J. J. (2023). Clava Cairns. World History Encyclopedia. https://www.worldhistory.org/Clava_Cairns/#google_vignette

Pilgrimage. (n.d.). https://www.whithorn.com/origins/pilgrimage/

Scott, & Scott. (2023, March 14). What is Scottish Witchcraft (or not)? – the role of the wise women. The Cailleach's Herbarium. https://theCailleachs-herbarium.com/2015/09/what-is-scottish-witchcraft-or-not-the-role-of-the-wise-women/#:~:text=Witchcraft%20in%20Scotland%20was%20known,to%20a%20%E2%80%9Cfoolish%20women%E2%80%9D

Scottish legends: The Cu Sith. (n.d.). Folkrealm Studies. https://folkrealmstudies.weebly.com/scottish-legends-the-cu-sith.html#google_vignette

Smith, K. (2019, April 3). 10 of the most wicked witches in Scottish history. Scottish Field. https://www.scottishfield.co.uk/culture/10-of-the-most-wicked-witches-in-scottish-history/

St. Ninian. (n.d.). https://www.whithorn.com/origins/st-ninian/

The horrifying execution of William Wallace. (n.d.). Mercat Tours Ltd, Edinburgh, Scotland. https://www.mercattours.com/blog-post/the-horrifying-execution-of-william-wallace

The Kelpie, mythical Scottish water horse. (2017, August 26). Historic UK. https://www.historic-uk.com/CultureUK/The-Kelpie/

The mystery of the miniature coffins. (n.d.). National Museums Scotland. https://www.nms.ac.uk/explore-our-collections/stories/scottish-history-and-archaeology/mystery-of-the-miniature-coffins/

The mystery of the miniature coffins. (n.d.). National Museums Scotland. https://www.nms.ac.uk/explore-our-collections/stories/scottish-history-and-archaeology/mystery-of-the-miniature-coffins/

9 798887 654379